Eco-Women
Protectors of the Earth

Willow Ann Sirch

fulcrum kids
GOLDEN, COLORADO

For Jim Sirch
husband, naturalist, teacher, friend

Copyright © 1996 Willow Ann Sirch

Book design by Alyssa Pumphrey

Cover photographs appear courtesy of (clockwise from top left): Rachel Carson and puppy, copyright © 1996 Shirley Briggs/Rachel Carson History Project; Katharine Payne, copyright © 1996 Katharine Payne; Barbara Kerr and sister, copyright © 1996 Barbara Kerr; Wangari Maathai receiving the Right Livelihood Award, copyright © 1996 Goldman Environmental Prize.

Library of Congress Cataloging-in-Publication Data

Sirch, Willow Ann.
    Eco-women : protectors of the earth / Willow Ann Sirch.
        p.   cm.
    Includes index.
    Summary: Presents brief biographies of women from different parts of the world who, singly and in groups, have made contributions to environmental protection.
    ISBN 1-55591-252-4 (pbk.)
    1. Women environmentalists—Biography—Juvenile literature. [1. Environmentalists.
2. Women—Biography.] I. Title.
GE55.S57   1996
333.7'16'0922—dc20
[B]   96-13380
                                         CIP
                                         AC

Printed in the United States of America

0 9 8 7 6 5 4 3 2 1

Fulcrum Publishing
350 Indiana Street, Suite 350
Golden, Colorado 80401-5093
(800) 992-2908 • (303) 277-1623

TABLE OF CONTENTS

ACKNOWLEDGMENTS

Just as it takes a whole village to raise a child, according to the African proverb, so it takes a small community to create a book. I would like to thank the following individuals and groups who have provided me with substantial assistance. Most importantly, I would like to thank the women who are the subjects of this book for taking time out from their busy schedules to review chapter drafts and offer their comments: Marjory Stoneman Douglas, Jane Goodall, Barbara Kerr, Katy Payne, Mardy Murie and Wangari Maathai. Special thanks are due Martha Hubbert on behalf of Marjory Stoneman Douglas and Bonnie Kreps on behalf of Mardy Murie. I am most grateful to Patricia A. Forkan, Executive Vice President of The Humane Society of the United States, for her insightful preface. My thanks also go to Kristin Mosher of the Jane Goodall Institute and Lauraine Schallop of Air-India. I very much appreciate assistance received from the Rachel Carson Council, Friends of the Everglades, Na Bolom, Solar Cookers International, the Wilderness Society, the Green Belt Movement, the Right Livelihood Award, and the Goldman Environmental Prize. I would like to take this opportunity to thank my parents, Bill and Shirley Soltow, and my grandmother, Helen Martin, for instilling in me values of compassion and responsibility toward the Earth and its animals, which has resulted in both this book and a fascinating career as a writer. As always, I am grateful to my good friend Emily Jayne Duckworth for her unflagging encouragement—especially in the dark days of first drafts. Finally, thanks go to my husband Jim, to whom this book is dedicated, for countless insights offered from a naturalist's perspective and for his steadfast support.

PREFACE

In 1973, I was among the first group of dreamers who set out to save the world's great whales. It started as a simple idea, that these magnificent, gentle giants should be safe from cruel harpoons. What I could not dream then was that now, 23 years later, although we have achieved much protection for whales, we're still fighting. The lesson: often a simple idea that seems right, and clear as a bell, becomes hostage to forces beyond our control, to the political and economic realities of a community or nation. But if we continue to believe, and pursue, we will prevail.

That the women profiled in this wonderful book had the courage to forge their own dreams for a better world, and continue to fight for them no matter what the obstacles, is testament to the fact that each of us can make a difference.

I have come to know these women, some of them personally and some through their work. Individually and collectively, they have helped to change the course of the planet and its wild inhabitants forever. As you come to know them, through their stories in this book, you will be moved and inspired to believe that you, too, have the power within you to find your simple idea, your goal, your dream—and make it come true.

—Patricia A. Forkan
Executive Vice President
The Humane Society of the United States

Eco-Women

Protectors of the Earth

Rachel Carson as a child, reading to her dog, Candy. Copyright © Shirley A. Briggs/Rachel Carson History Project. Used by permission of the Rachel Carson History Project.

Chapter One

THE QUIET COURAGE OF RACHEL CARSON

"… man is a part of nature and his war against nature is inevitably a war against himself."

—*Rachel Carson*

It was a cool, misty autumn night. Black waves battered the cold rocks of the Maine shore. Each crash brought a fresh blast of wet, salty sea air. A crab scuttled along the dark beach. A woman in late middle age walked along the shore. She lovingly carried a bundled blanket in her arms as she climbed over the rocks. Stopping at the water's edge, she pulled the folds of the blanket away from the face of a baby. Just as she did so, an enormous wave crashed against the rocky shore, spraying white foam high into the air. The baby laughed. So did the woman. He was meeting the ocean for the first time. She had spent a lifetime studying the secrets of the sea. The differences in their age and experience melted away at the edge of the roaring surf, and the two were united by their delight in the dark, mysterious power of the ocean.

When she was born in Springdale, Pennsylvania, Rachel Carson was an unlikely candidate to become a marine biologist. Her home was hundreds of miles from the sea. And, in the year 1907, scientific jobs were all but closed to women. Indeed, women could not even vote in national elections.

Rachel's family included her parents, her older brother Robert and older sister Marian. She grew up in a farmhouse on 65 acres of woodland and meadow. It was an island of nature surrounded by "progress." Coal mines, steel mills, aluminum plants, iron works, glass factories and chemical

3

manufacturers were all around. But on the Carson family land, nature was just waiting to be explored.

Beyond the back door was the apple orchard. Rachel used to walk here with her father. In spring, she climbed the trees, taking care not to disturb the nests of baby robins. They fascinated her with their tightly shut eyes and hungry open beaks. In summer, she lay on her back in sunny meadows full of daisies and buttercups and watched butterflies drift from flower to flower. She listened to the chorus of buzzing and clicking insects 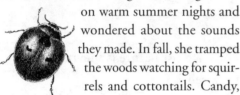 on warm summer nights and wondered about the sounds they made. In fall, she tramped the woods watching for squirrels and cottontails. Candy, her dog, often kept her company. Sometimes at dusk they would startle a young raccoon or a waddling opossum on its way to find food. In later years, Rachel remembered herself as a child spending "long days out of doors in fields and woods, happiest with the wild birds and creatures as companions."[1]

Did Rachel's mother play a part in developing her daughter's love of nature? Perhaps. Certainly, Maria Carson enjoyed a sense of kinship with all life. She encouraged Rachel to listen to the birds singing, to go for walks in the woods and meadows. When an insect was trapped in her kitchen, she took the time to release it back outside. Her young daughter watched and remembered.

A coal company once offered to pay the Carson family for the right to dig a tunnel under their farm. The tunnel would not affect the appearance of the land above it, the company promised. It was during the depression—the Carsons needed the money. But, no, said Rachel's father, the land was too important to take chances. Later, he suspected the mining company of going ahead with the digging without his permission—but there was no way to prove it. Rachel learned to cherish the land as her parents did. Perhaps she also learned not to believe everything promised by large and wealthy companies.

While in the fourth grade, Rachel had her first story published in *St. Nicholas*—a popular children's magazine. Her story was about a military pilot. She sent it in just as the United States was about to enter World War I in 1917. The magazine sent her an award of ten dollars. Looking back as an adult, Rachel would say, "I doubt that any royalty check of recent years has given me as great joy as the notice of that award."[2] The recognition set her on the writer's path.

Although Rachel's home was far from any seacoast, she was always fascinated by the ocean. She loved adventure stories about pirates, sea voyages and mysterious marine creatures. Finding factual information about the ocean, however, was more of a challenge. Until the early twentieth century, little was known about the ocean's depths or the animals that lived there. That began to change about the time Rachel was growing up in Springdale.

In the 1930s and 1940s, early divers were tied to their ship by an air hose that allowed them to breathe. They wore heavy equipment. Movement was limited. Later, Jacques Cousteau changed all that. In the 1950s, he developed a way for a diver to carry a tank of air on his or her back. This made exploring much easier. Such changes in marine research would be eagerly followed by Rachel Carson all her life.

Rachel's school years flew by. With her family's encouragement and the help of a scholarship, she entered Pennsylvania College for Women (later renamed Chatham College). Her major was English.

While at Chatham, Rachel took a biology course with an exciting young teacher. Mary Scott Skinker made the natural world come alive for Rachel. Her growing understanding of the science of living things gave Rachel even more appreciation for the out-of-doors she had loved as a child.

Rachel decided to switch her major to biology. Most of her professors were against it. They were being practical. Women were accepted in the world of writing, but not in the world of science. There were virtually no scientific jobs for women and no teaching positions other than at a few women's colleges.

It did not matter. Rachel loved what she was learning too much to give it up. It did not occur to her at this point that she might combine writing with a scientific career. In 1929 she graduated *magna cum laude* (with high honors). She was awarded a full scholarship to study marine zoology at Johns Hopkins University in Baltimore, Maryland.

Rachel spent part of the summer before graduate school working at the famous Woods Hole Marine Biological Laboratory on Cape Cod. She finally saw the ocean for the first time! Woods Hole meant listening to waves, watching shorebirds and clambering along rocky shores to examine seaweed and tidal pools. At college, her interest in marine biology had set her apart. Here, she was joined by scientists who shared her passion for the ocean.

Summer passed all too quickly. In the fall, Rachel stopped off in Washington, D.C., on the way to her studies at Johns Hopkins. She wanted to speak to Elmer Higgins. He was one of the department heads at the Bureau of Fisheries (later renamed the U.S. Fish and Wildlife Service). She wanted to learn what opportunities might be open to her after graduate school.

The answer? There were no jobs for women in science—not in business, not at museums. Higgins was sympathetic, but could offer little hope. Rachel might get a job at a government agency like the one he worked for, he suggested, but the government was not hiring just then.

Rachel went on to Johns Hopkins. The year was 1929. Within two months, the stock market crashed. The Great Depression had arrived. Factories and businesses closed. Millions of people lost their jobs. Many students were forced to give up their studies. Rachel was lucky. Her full scholarship meant that she could stay in school.

During the depression, it was common for families to share housing and expenses. Rachel's parents came to live with her in her tiny apartment. Before long, they were joined by her brother Robert who, like so many, was out of work.

Rachel received her master's degree in 1932. Then, for two years, she got along with part-time work at Johns Hopkins. In July 1935, her father died suddenly of a heart attack. While mourning her father, she realized it would now be up to her to support herself and her mother. She would have to find full-time work.

Rachel decided to pay another visit to Elmer Higgins at the Bureau of Fisheries. By now, the nation's economy was beginning to improve. President Herbert Hoover had been replaced by Franklin Delano Roosevelt. Under Roosevelt's New Deal, thousands were given jobs to build roads, bridges and buildings funded by the government. His Civilian Conservation Corps created hiking trails, maintained parks and protected nature.

Things were changing for women, too. Eleanor Roosevelt, the president's charismatic wife, was very popular. She spoke in favor of women's rights. The president himself appointed the first woman to hold a cabinet post when he made Frances Perkins the secretary of labor.

Elmer Higgins offered to let Rachel try writing scripts for a radio program. The show, "Romance Under the Waters," was jokingly referred to as "Seven-Minute Fish Tales" by the rest of the office staff. Higgins liked her first script, and she was hired. At a time when many people were out of work, Rachel had a job.

The job, however, meant more than money. Until now, Rachel had not realized that she could combine her studies in marine biology with her love of the written word. She thought she had given that up when she changed her major from English to biology. She now knew that by becoming a biologist she had not closed the door on her writing; she had merely given herself something to write about.

While working on radio scripts, Rachel got a big break. The Bureau of Fisheries announced an opening for a junior aquatic biologist. An exam would be offered. The person with the highest score would get the job. In those days many women were turned down for jobs even when they were more qualified than the men who applied. At one interview after another, women heard the same discouraging words, "Sorry, we gave the job to a man because he has a family to support." It did not matter that plenty of women, Rachel included, had family members to support!

Rachel took the exam and earned the highest score. Elmer Higgins requested that she be assigned to his department. She had done what her professors had feared no woman could do! She had landed a full-time job as a marine scientist. This personal victory came just in time. That same year, Rachel's older sister Marian died, leaving two young daughters. Marjorie and Virginia came to live with Rachel and her mother. Rachel was a second mother to her sister's children—and the sole support of her nieces and mother.

After the radio scripts, Rachel was asked to write an article about the sea. She worked on it carefully. Finally, she handed it in to her boss. Upon reading it, Higgins sighed and handed it back. "I don't think this will do," he said. But he was smiling. "Better try again," he told her. "But, this one might make a good article for the *Atlantic*."

Rachel could hardly believe it. The *Atlantic* was a prestigious magazine. Eventually, she took her boss's advice and sent it in. When her story was accepted, it launched her career as a freelance nature writer.

One thing led to another. An editor at Simon and Schuster saw Rachel's article in the *Atlantic*. He wrote, asking if she would consider doing a book. Rachel decided to try. She researched and wrote on weekends and late evenings after work. She found that writing a book while holding down a job was difficult. It was also a solitary business. "Writing is a lonely occupation at best," Rachel once lamented.[3] How did she cope with loneliness? Her cats were a big help. Rachel always had a special feeling for cats and their quiet company. She once wrote "Cats are

extremely sensitive to the joys and sorrows of their human friends. …"[4]

It is easy to imagine Rachel working late into the night, absorbed by her subject. Books lie open on a nearby table. Her desk is covered with papers and articles. In the middle of one of the paper piles, a cat lies curled, asleep. Once, as Rachel labored over the draft of her first book, she made a sketch in the margin of her beloved cat Buzzie.

Under the Sea-Wind was published in 1941. It told the story of a seacoast. Rachel wrote as if the sea were a stage and the animals and plants were players, each with a role to perform. She showed how the lives of the different animals—including humans—depended on one another and on the land where they all lived. No one had ever written a book quite like it before.

Sadly, Rachel's first book received little attention. It came out shortly before the United States entered World War II. People were focused on the war, not the wonders of nature.

Ten years passed before Rachel completed her next book, *The Sea Around Us*. Where her earlier book had told a story, this new book presented a straightforward picture of the ocean, its history and its importance to all life on Earth. It was an immediate success. *The Sea Around Us* was a Book-of-the Month Club selection. It stayed on the *New York Times'* best-seller list for 81 weeks. Rachel received the National Book Award and two colleges awarded her honorary doctorates.

Rachel's next book, *The Edge of the Sea*, was also successful. It told about the tidal zone where the ocean meets the shore. Bob Hines, an illustrator from the agency where Rachel worked, was hired to do the art. As Hines recalled: "We'd go out on the mudflats. She'd scrounge around to find what she wanted. We'd bring the stuff back in a bucket and I'd make the drawings. Then Rachel would put them back in the bucket and return them to their natural places on the beach."[5] Like her mother, who had returned insects she found in the house to the outdoors, Rachel Carson believed in respecting the lives of all creatures.

Thanks to a grant, Rachel had been able to take time off from her job without pay to finish the book. As her book sales rocketed, she decided to return the grant money. There were others who needed it more.

The money also meant Rachel could quit her job and build a cottage for herself and her mother on the beautiful coast of Maine. Everywhere she went, Rachel was famous. People pointed her out, asked for her autograph, complimented her books. A quiet, private person, Rachel found the publicity difficult. She was more at home in wet sneakers facing a beach full of gulls than in high heels before an admiring public. Soon, she would take on her last book and her greatest challenge.

It all began with a letter from a woman named Olga Owens Huckins. The year was 1957. A plane had sprayed pesticide over the town where Huckins lived. That day, she found seven dead songbirds in her yard. The passing of each day brought more dead birds. Once, she watched horrified as a robin suddenly dropped from its perch in a tree. The deadly pesticide was DDT.

DDT stands for dichloro-diphenyl-trichloroethane. Hailed at first as a miracle, it proved to be anything but. It killed animals it was not meant to kill. It was suspected of causing cancer in people and animals.

Some animals, like the birds in Huckins's garden, were killed outright. Others were

Many kinds of birds, including robins, were harmed by the use of DDT. Copyright © Luther C. Goldman/U.S. Fish and Wildlife Service.

affected in other ways. For instance, DDT kept some birds from producing eggshells strong enough to protect the young inside. The eggshells broke easily. Birds died before they could even hatch. Some kinds of birds, such as osprey, bald eagles and peregrine falcons, nearly became extinct.

As a scientist and one of the country's best-loved nature writers, Rachel wanted to help. But it was a difficult time for her to take on another writing project. Like Rachel's sister years before, Rachel's niece Marjorie had recently died. She left behind a five-year-old son, Roger, whom Rachel adopted. There was also Rachel's ninety-year-old mother to care for. And, Rachel herself was unwell. She suffered from arthritis, sinus trouble and a stomach ulcer.

She thought of the many animals she had watched and wondered about over the years. She remembered the shorebirds, the tiny sea creatures and the woods where she had walked as a child. She realized that everything she held dear as a naturalist was in danger. Despite her troubles, she chose to go ahead with the book. "If I didn't at least try," she said, "I could never again be happy in nature."[6]

During 1958, while Rachel was researching her book, her mother died. Rachel was overcome with grief. Her mother had been a loving friend, sharing her daughter's life and work. It was Maria Carson who had typed the final drafts of all of Rachel's books.

Rachel Carson watches migrating hawks at Hawk Mountain, Pennsylvania, 1945. Copyright © Shirley A. Briggs/Rachel Carson History Project. Used by permission of the Rachel Carson History Project.

After months of grieving, Rachel finally struggled back to work. She thought of how pleased her mother would have been to see this new book published. She worked hard, even after learning that she had cancer. This meant surgery and radiation therapy—which made work on the book go more slowly still. Even so, Rachel kept on. *Silent Spring* was published in 1962. It was dedicated to Dr. Albert Schweitzer, the great humanitarian who believed in "Reverence for Life" and who spent his life helping people and animals. *Silent Spring* forever changed the way people would think about nature.

The making of chemical pesticides was a multimillion-dollar industry. By showing that pesticides were dangerous, Rachel was a threat to the industry—and the industry fought back. Spokespeople for the chemical industry said that pesticides were perfectly safe. When that did not work, they tried to discredit Rachel Carson. They said she was not a real scientist. They charged that, as a woman, she was foolish and sentimental. They said she cared more about nature than about people. Quietly, calmly, Rachel answered their attacks.

She explained how pesticides travel through the water supply, how they remain in the soil, how they enter food chains and poison people as well as animals. Many people listened. One of them was President John F. Kennedy. He had his Science Advisory Committee study pesticide use in the United States. In time, the committee's report agreed with Rachel Carson's findings. It paved the way for new laws that would control the use of many pesticides.

Near the end of her life, Rachel Carson was very ill—too ill, in fact, to accept in person the many honors and awards that came to be showered upon her. She died at her home on April 14, 1964. As a writer, she was pleased to think that, through her books, she would "live on even in the minds of many who do not know me."[7] Today, environmentalists everywhere continue to be inspired by her. Through their efforts to protect animals and nature, they echo the spirit and courage of Rachel Carson.

WHAT YOU CAN DO

1. Learn more about the work of Rachel Carson by reading *Rachel Carson: The Wonder of Nature* by Catherine Reef, illustrated by Larry Raymond (New York: Twenty-First Century Books, 1991).

2. If you live near a beach, help out during the annual National Beach Clean-up. For information on what you can do to help, write to the National Oceanic and Atmospheric Administration's Marine Debris Information Office, The Center for Marine Conservation, 1725 DeSales Street NW, Washington, DC 20036. Ask about their free ocean information packet for students.

3. Learn more about the ocean and its ecosystems. One good book is *Exploring An Ocean Tide Pool* by Jeanne Bendick (New York: Henry Holt and Co., 1992). Another

resource is the publication *Dolphin Log* published by the Cousteau Society. For information on getting a sample copy or subscribing, write to Dolphin Log, 930 West 21st Street, Norfolk, VA 23517.

4. Check that the dish and laundry soaps your family uses are biodegradable. It should say this on the label. You can find biodegradable soaps in many grocery and health food stores. Another good source is Seventh Generation. You can get their catalog by writing to them at 49 Hercules Drive, Colchester, VT 05446.

5. Cut up all six-pack rings before throwing them away. They can harm many kinds of animals including seabirds and fish. Also, never release helium balloons. They can travel many miles. If they come down in the ocean, they may be eaten by sea turtles and other animals that mistake them for jellyfish. Balloons can hurt or even kill animals that eat them.

6. Support the work of the Rachel Carson Council, 8940 Jones Mill Road, Chevy Chase, MD 20815.

Marjory Stoneman Douglas at age one and a half. Copyright © Florida State Archives.

Chapter Two
MARJORY STONEMAN DOUGLAS AND THE RIVER OF GRASS

"One can do so much by reading, learning, and talking to people!"
—*Marjory Stoneman Douglas*

The year was 1915. A young Massachusetts woman boarded the train bound for Florida. In those days, it was unusual to see a woman traveling alone. Most passengers took brief note and returned to their books, their newspapers or conversations.

At the journey's end, the young woman got her first glimpse of Miami. It was not much to look at. Just a scruffy boom town. Plots of land with For Sale signs on them were everywhere. A scattering of buildings was going up. The finished houses were plain, squat and shoddily built. Rude gaps showed in the landscape where trees had been cleared to prepare for more building, leaving scrubby brush and broken stumps. There was quick money to be made in Miami real estate.

But Miami could wait. Something more pressing was on the young woman's mind. Eagerly, she scanned the crowd on the platform. She had not seen her father in twenty years. Which was he? Actually, it was her father who spotted her first. "Hello, sweetheart," he said, and kissed her. The two were reunited "with no fuss and feathers," as the young woman, Marjory Stoneman Douglas, would later recall. And with that, she was ready to tackle Miami.

Today, Marjory's name is usually linked with the state that became her home. Like many Floridians, however, she was not born there. Instead, she adopted Florida and her great love for her state's natural beauty prompted her to become its most famous and well-loved environmentalist.

Marjory Stoneman was born in Minnesota in 1890. Her parents were Lillian and Frank Stoneman. Her father's business failed when Marjory was three and the family moved to Providence, Rhode Island. Marjory's earliest memories include hearing delightful strains of piano music as her mother played for friends and neighbors in the evening. She remembers sitting in her mother's lap at night watching the stars and being read to by her father. When Marjory was four, the family visited Florida. Marjory loved the state's brilliant, white, tropical light. She never forgot this first impression.

Frank Stoneman's business ventures failed again and the family had to move once more, this time within Providence. In time, living on the edge took its toll on Marjory's mother. Spells of anxiety led, finally, to a mental breakdown. Soon after, Marjory's parents separated. Marjory was six. She and her mother went to live in Taunton, Massachusetts with her mother's parents and sister.

All was not peaceful in Marjory's new household. Her mother's health did not improve. The family blamed Marjory's father for her mother's illness. Marjory made up her own mind even then. She did not believe the bitter things her relatives said about Frank Stoneman. It was a stressful time.

Marjory often sought escape in books. Throughout school, reading and writing were her strongest subjects. She wrote stories and had a word puzzle published in *St. Nicholas*—a magazine for children.

At a time when many women were not educated beyond high school, Marjory attended Wellesley College just outside Bos-

The Everglades is home to roseate spoonbills (pictured here), egrets and many other waterbirds. Copyright © U.S. Fish and Wildlife Service.

ton. Here, Marjory's interest in reading and writing remained strong. She also enjoyed her speech classes.

Marjory graduated in 1912. Her excitement at graduating was overshadowed by painful news. Her mother was dying of cancer. Lillian Stoneman passed away weeks later. After her mother's death, Marjory felt lonely and confused about what to do. She worked for a time at a department store. When Kenneth Douglas asked her to marry him, she could think of no reason not to do so.

The marriage was not a happy one. Douglas was thirty years older than Marjory. Before long, he was jailed for writing bad checks. Marjory felt she did not really even know the man she had married. She wanted a divorce.

Meanwhile, Marjory's father had moved to Miami and started the newspaper that was to become the *Miami Herald*. Upon hearing of his wife's death, he had remarried. To speed along her own divorce, Marjory decided to go live with her father and stepmother.

In those days Miami's "houses looked as if they had just been dropped like a load of boxes on cleared lots."[1] Yet, just outside the city, the land was an exotic, untouched jungle. Palm trees of all sorts and sizes mingled with tangled vines, lacy Spanish moss and strange-looking air plants. The land was very different from her former New England home.

Marjory soon had a job as a reporter on her father's newspaper. Frank Stoneman was not afraid to say what was on his mind. His opinions were progressive—and often shared by his daughter. Father and daughter, for instance, were among the few to speak out against Governor Napoleon Bonaparte Broward's popular plan for draining the Everglades.

The Everglades, at the southern tip of Florida, is a huge, wild area of grassy swampland. Many of its animals are endangered or threatened. The Seminole Indians found safety in its dense, green depths when threatened by whites in the 1800s. Here, shy roseate spoonbills dabble for food in knee-deep water. Manatees gently drift along canals, and tiny crabs poke among the tangled roots of mangrove trees.

Alligators, active at night, doze in the bright sun. There is no place quite like it. As Marjory says, "there is no other Everglades in the world."[2]

In Frank Stoneman's day, as today, land development was big business. Most people saw the Everglades as a worthless swamp. If it were drained, the land could provide useful things, they said, like farms and homes and shopping centers. Why should it be saved, they argued, for the sake of a few alligators? The Everglades seemed like such a big place, it was hard for people to realize how quickly it could disappear. Yet, it *was* disappearing.

Marjory was quickly drawn into the debate over draining what remained of the Everglades. She and her father were ahead of their time. In an age when most people gave little thought to protecting the environment, Marjory and her father had strong ideas about saving the swampy region.

Florida panthers are among the many threatened and endangered species found in the Everglades. Copyright © U.S. Fish and Wildlife Service.

15

The United States entered World War I in 1917. Suddenly there was little time in Marjory's life for the Everglades. She spent a year in the Navy and then traveled to France with the Red Cross. When the war was over, she returned to Florida—but not before she had seen some of the great cities of Europe like Paris, Venice and Athens. The memory of their beauty shaped her dreams for her own hometown city.

After the war, Marjory continued writing for the newspaper for eleven years. Then she decided to try something different. She left her job and devoted herself to freelance writing. She wrote short stories for magazines like *The Saturday Evening Post* and *Ladies' Home Journal*. The Everglades often played a part in her stories. One was about the dangerous journey across the Everglades made by an old man and a young boy. Another was about a man who lost his life trying to protect his land from poachers.

Marjory's writing career was a success. Before long, she could afford to buy her own cozy, one-room house. (She lives there to this day!) Her lifestyle was simple—and that is how she wanted it. Even though she had her own place, she remained close to her family. After her father died at the age of 84, Marjory continued to see her stepmother regularly until Lilla Stoneman's death years later.

Marjory continued writing and living in her one-room house in much the same way for sixteen years. She still cared about the Everglades. In fact, she helped out with a group that was trying to get the Everglades declared a national park. Neither the public nor the government, however, had paid much attention. Then something happened that would change Marjory's life—and the Everglades—forever.

The year was 1942. Overseas, the world seemed to be falling apart. World War II raged in Europe. At home, there was rationing of gas, sugar, coffee and other items. Otherwise, however, life went on pretty much as usual. An editor named Hervey Allen was working on a series of books about American rivers. He wanted Marjory to write about the Miami River. This idea made her laugh. "You can't write about the Miami River," she told him. "It's only about an inch long."[3]

Then Marjory had an idea. Why not write about the Everglades instead? Allen agreed. For Marjory, the decision would result in more than a book topic. The Everglades would become her life's work. She was 52.

Marjory began by seeking the advice of a scientist. Garald Parker was a water specialist for the state of Florida. He explained that it was incorrect to call the Everglades a "swamp." A swamp is an area of standing water. The water of the Everglades is always moving.

Could the Everglades be called *a river of grass*? Marjory asked. Parker agreed that it could. Marjory liked this way of thinking about the Everglades so well that she used it as the title of her book. By coining the phrase "river of grass," she forever changed the way people would think of the Everglades. No longer a still, stagnant swamp, it was seen as the lively ecosystem it is.

Marjory's book *The Everglades: River of Grass* was published in 1947. It presented the area's history. It showed that the Everglades was a home to many animals. It also demonstrated how people depended on the Everglades for water. As Marjory explained in her book "The Everglades evaporate, the moisture goes up into the clouds, the clouds are blown to the north, and the rain comes down over the Kissimmee River and Lake Okeechobee."[4] The process was like a big circle. Eventually, runoff from the lake ended up back in the Everglades.

People began to see that their own lives were linked with that of this beautiful ecosystem. In the same year in which her book appeared, Everglades National Park was formally opened by President Harry Truman. Although the park covered only a small part of the entire Everglades region, it was a start. Marjory was pleased.

It might seem as though the struggle to save "the Glades" was nearly won. Sadly, that was far from the truth. In years to follow, the U.S. Army Corps of Engineers dug many miles of canals in the Everglades, built dams and put in floodgates. They "improved" the Kissimmee River by straightening its course. For centuries, the Kissimmee River had gently wandered in a roundabout way, bringing life-giving water and marsh habitat to much of central Florida. It was turned into a long, lifeless ditch.

"Progress" proved a disaster to both the Kissimmee River and the Everglades. Water levels dropped. Pesticides from surrounding farms and ranches polluted the waterways. Many animals died. Farmers chipped away, bit by bit, at what undeveloped land was left. To top it off, a huge jetport was scheduled to be built near the park, threatening wildlife with noise and pollution.

Finally, people had had enough. Angry protesters stopped the huge bulldozers that came

Marjory Stoneman Douglas is joined by one of her feline friends as she sits on the steps of her one-room bungalow. Copyright © Florida State Archives.

to level the ground for the jetport. One of them was Joe Browder of the National Audubon Society. He asked Marjory to help in the fight against the jetport. She answered that one person could not do much alone. He suggested that she start an organization—and that is just what she did.

Marjory was 78 years old when she began the organization Friends of the Everglades. But she was still a fighter—and she had found something worth fighting for. Those speech classes she had taken in college now came in handy.

Marjory began speaking to any group that would listen. At a time of life when most people are thinking about retirement, she was "on the road." She traveled throughout south and central Florida, speaking to civic groups, conservation groups, school children, bird watchers, town meetings and planning commissioners. She became known as the little old lady with the big floppy hat. She faced angry crowds of landowners, explaining why they could not build on the land they had purchased. She spoke in terms that people could understand—describing the Everglades as if it were the circulatory system of a person's body. It had to keep flowing, she told people, or the whole system would break down. She helped people see that saving the Everglades was more than just a nice thing to do—it meant the survival of southern Florida.

Each time she spoke, more people joined her organization. In the first year, she had 500 members. By the end of the second year, there were 1,000. In time, Friends of the Everglades would have thousands of members from 38 different states.

The jetport project was abandoned. Marjory's Army, as her group was known, had won a major victory. But the battle for the Everglades was not yet over. Throughout the 1970s and 1980s, Marjory continued her speaking career. Wherever development threatened a part of the Everglades ecosystem, Marjory was sure to be found. Even the gradual loss of her eyesight did not stop her. "No matter how poor my eyes are, I can still talk!" Marjory would say. "I'll talk about the Everglades at the drop of a hat. Whoever wants me to talk, I'll come over and tell them about preserving the Everglades. Sometimes, I tell them more than they wanted to know!"[5]

In the late 1970s, the South Florida Water Management Board decided to return the Kissimmee River to its original path. The work of the U.S. Army Corps of Engineers was undone and the river returned to its meandering route. Many acres of land have been added to the Everglades National Park. Some drained areas have been restored. Some restrictions have

For ages, people have celebrated animals in art, while destroying the places where animals live. These alligators are from an ancient Roman mosaic. Copyright © Dr. Emily Jayne Duckworth.

been placed on farming practices that pollute the waters of the Everglades.

What about Marjory? In 1975, she was named Conservationist of the Year by the Florida Audubon Society. She received the same honor from the Florida Wildlife Federation one year later. In 1989, she was made honorary vice president of the Sierra Club. Her story has appeared in articles in nature publications as well as popular magazines like *Time, People* and *Esquire*.

At 106 years old, Marjory Stoneman Douglas is still a voice for the Everglades. Her secretary, Martha Hubbert, assists her in answering mail from around the world. Marjory records her responses on audiocassette tapes. These are sent to writers, conservationists and others in answer to their questions about the Everglades.

What message does Marjory Stoneman Douglas have for young people? "Find out what needs to be done and do it!" she says.[6] Can kids make a difference for the Earth?

"One can do so much," observes Marjory, "by reading, learning, and talking to people. Students need to learn all they can about animals and the environment. Most of all, they need to share what they have learned."[7]

Marjory Stoneman Douglas became active in protecting the Everglades at an age when many people are thinking about retirement. Copyright © Florida State Archives.

WHAT YOU CAN DO

1. Learn more about the life and work of Marjory Stoneman Douglas by reading *Marjory Stoneman Douglas: Voice of the Everglades* by Jennifer Bryant (Frederick, MD: Twenty-first Century Books, 1991).

2. Adopt an endangered manatee. For information on how to go about it, write to the Save the Manatee Club at 1101 Audubon Way, Maitland, FL 32751.

3. Learn about the Everglades and the Seminole Indians who live nearby through the story of a young girl named Billie Wind. Read *The Talking Earth* by Jean Craighead George (New York: Harper & Row, 1983).

4. Support the work of Friends of the Everglades, 3744 Stewart Avenue, Coconut Grove, FL 33133.

Young Gertrude Blom about the time she went to Mexico. Copyright © Na Bolom.

Chapter Three

GERTRUDE BLOM AND THE LACANDON RAIN FOREST

"The memories of the singing birds, the exquisite colors of the vegetation, and the beautiful rivers come back to my mind like echoes from the past … the time has come for us to wake up to what we are doing and take steps to stop this destruction."

—*Gertrude Blom*

It is morning. A young Lacandon Indian woman awakes. She has long black hair and wears a white tunic, the traditional dress of her people worn by both men and women. The thatched roof of her family's home keeps out the misty morning air of the rain forest. A fire smolders in the middle of the room. Bags of vegetables and leaf-wrapped packages of salt and dried gourds hang high above her head suspended from the smoke-blackened roof. Around her, her family remains sleeping in their string hammocks.

The young woman knows it is morning by the way the sun tumbles through the open doorway, by the way it reaches in through the wooden slats of the walls of her house. She rises and goes outside. Chickens scratch softly in the dust of the clearing that surrounds the little group of thatched homes. On either side of the houses are small vegetable gardens and old corn patches. Beyond the clearing, orchids and air plants cling to the towering trees. Beneath the branches and hidden from view are ancient stone carvings half-covered by dark green moss and tangled vines. They were made hundreds of years ago by the girl's ancestors and they portray some of the gods worshipped by her people. Nearby, a bright green parrot squawks noisily. There is a crackling of broken twigs as a wild pig is startled in his search for food. Otherwise, it is quiet in the early morning light.

Suddenly, in the distance, the buzz of a chain saw is heard. A team of loggers has arrived for work. They are here to cut down the hard, rich mahogany and cedar trees to be sold and shipped overseas. Their work will leave great gaps in the rich forest landscape. The girl is surprised to hear them. They have never entered this far into the land of the Lacandon Indians before. What will her people do, where will they go, she wonders, when the rain forest that is their home is gone?

Gertrude Blom met the Lacandon Indians for the first time when she was a young woman herself. She was born Gertrude Elizabeth Loertscher in Bern, Switzerland, in 1901. She and her brother and sister were the children of a Jewish mother and Protestant minister father. So, from the beginning, her life was shaped by an acceptance of different ways of thinking and doing. School bored young Trudi, but the world of nature fascinated her. Among her favorite books were those by a German author named Carl May that featured American Indians. His main character, Karl, tried to protect the Indians from people who wanted to cheat them or "civilize" them. Inspired by the sto-

ries, Trudi and her friends would play at being Indians themselves after school.

As a child, Trudi, like many children, was often afraid of the dark. Her strong nature revealed itself when she decided to do something about it. As she later recalled:

> One day I decided … that I could not be scared anymore. I forced myself to go to the graveyard … on the edge of the forest near the town. The first time I went halfway and ran back frightened to death. Every evening I went a little farther until I could go to the cemetery. I would imagine skeletons on my back and run home. Finally, I was able to stay, without fear, until it was dark, and walk calmly home to go to bed.[1]

Trudi and her family lived in an apartment in Bern. Below them lived Herr Duby, an official in the trade union for Swiss railway workers. Young Kurt Duby was close to Trudi in age, and they became good friends. Together they attended radical union meetings. Trudi's conservative family strongly disapproved. But Trudi was very strong-willed. She refused to give up the meetings. Sadly, as time went on, she became estranged from her family.

As a young woman, Trudi studied horticulture and social work. She spent a year living in England in the home of a Quaker family. Their strong sense of justice appealed to her. Soon she became involved in public speaking. She also began writing articles for newspapers.

Upon returning to Switzerland, Trudi was married to Kurt Duby, but the marriage did not last. After that, she traveled to Germany where the Nazis were quickly gaining power. Trudi spoke out against them at public meetings. The meetings often turned violent. It was a dangerous time to be in Germany.

In 1933, Hitler was made chancellor of Germany. After that, efforts against the Nazis had to be carried out in secret. Trudi managed to get information to Swiss newspapers about Nazi cruelties. She was often in danger, but escape was not easy. Finally, she managed to get away. She went to live in France to continue her efforts to work against Nazism. In 1939, she came to the United States to raise money to help European refugees—people who had lost their homes because of war and political troubles. When she returned to France, the country had been taken over by the Nazis. Trudi was arrested and put into prison for five months. It was a painful and frightening time in her life. Finally, the Swiss government was able to get her released. By 1940, she had had enough of politics. The United States and all of Europe was at war. Tired and disillusioned, Trudi went to Mexico to live.

In Mexico, Trudi became interested in the women who worked in the factories. Their faces told of the hardships they had experienced. She told their story in news articles. For the first time, Trudi began taking photographs. She took pictures of many of the women she encountered. Even though she knew little about photography, Trudi's pictures had a haunting quality that made people look twice.

Trudi made her first visit to a Mexican rain forest in 1943. She described her experience years later:

> I fell in love with the jungle from the moment I first saw its … great trees and exotic plants … . I was held spellbound by the incredible musical sounds of the insects, from the highest notes to the lowest, and the singing of the frogs and all the hundreds of birds that I had never seen. I listened in amazement to the peculiar cry of the howler monkey and the deafening sound of the tapir crashing through the undergrowth like a tractor. I was transfixed by the enormous flocks of parrots and the macaws … a rainbow of colors in the sky. Then there were all the snakes of different colors slithering in between the fallen leaves on the floor of the jungle. I didn't feel any fear in the midst of this new environment … . This jungle filled me with a sense of wonder that has never left me.[2]

It was on this trip that she saw the Lacandon Indians for the first time. She was amazed at how they seemed to be one with their environment.

> I looked up and suddenly realized a man, one human being, was standing there on a log. I had not seen or heard him come up. He seemed to be a part of that log, standing totally immobile and erect and melting in to the forest. Finally … other Lacandones appeared … . With their clothes and hair and silent footsteps, they seemed really part of the jungle.[3]

The Lacandon Indians whom Trudi met lived in a rain forest in Chiapas. Perhaps the poorest state in Mexico, Chiapas is in the south of Mexico. The Lacandon rain forest borders the country of Guatemala. The Lacandones dressed in simple white tunics as their Mayan ancestors had done. They practiced the old, traditional ways of their people, living off the forest, never taking more than the land could spare. At about the time Trudi met them, the Lacandon Maya were beginning to experience major changes in their way of life. Thousands of

Lacandon boy in a dugout canoe. Copyright © Na Bolom.

Mexican peasants were moved into this region by their government. As the peasants' families grew, so did their need for food and land to grow it. The rain forest began being chipped away—for land for poor farmers, for cheap pasture to raise cattle and by loggers who wanted to cut and sell fine rain forest woods for profit.

That same year, 1943, Trudi met and married Franz Blom. He was a Danish explorer, mapmaker and archaeologist. He had earned a doctorate in Mayan culture at Harvard University. Together Trudi and Franz explored the rain forest, making treks into the jungle for as long as seven months at a time. They traveled by horse, by mule, by canoe and on foot. They charted the jungles and searched for Mayan ruins. Franz recorded their finds in a book that he wrote. Trudi took her haunting black-and-white photographs. In the course of their explorations, they developed a special feeling for the people of the Lacandon jungle and their history.

Between A.D. 300 and A.D. 900, large Mayan cities of white stone rose amid what is now the Lacandon rain forest and the lowland forests of Guatemala. Mystical priests worshipped within beautiful, pyramid-shaped temples with flattened roofs. Artisans carved *stelae* (freestanding stone monuments) with the portraits of fierce warriors. Nobles and priests lived in the cities. They were supported by the craftspeople, tradespeople and farmers who lived outside. In return for that support, the ruling class saw to the needs of the many Mayan gods and directed community affairs. Mayan culture included a written language in the form of hieroglyphics and a highly developed knowledge of astronomy and arithmetic. The Mayans had a wonderfully complex solar or sun-based calendar. (Ours is a lunar calendar, based on the Earth's movements in relation to the moon.)

The history of the ancient Maya is full of mysteries. Of the 800 or so Mayan hieroglyphics, only a little more than half have been deciphered. Why, scholars wonder, did the great civilization fall apart? Around A.D. 900, the priests and nobles left the cities. The building of the great temples and the carving of stone monuments stopped. One hundred years later, the center of Mayan culture had moved to another area. But some Maya stayed behind.

Six hundred years later, the descendants of the Maya in southern Chiapas suffered cruelly at the hands of the Spanish conquistadors. The Spanish brought illnesses unknown to this part of the world. Mayans who survived disease were forced into slavery. Some escaped to the rain forests. They were safe there. The Spaniards seldom followed. The Maya remained in the rain forest, living a traditional lifestyle. Their descendants, who live much as their ancestors did, are the Lacandon Indians. Today, modern deforestation may accomplish what the conquistadors were unable to do—wipe out the last of the Maya.

Eco-Women

The Lacandon rain forest, like others around the world, is being destroyed. Rain forests are cut down for wood, to grow crops and in some cases, to graze cattle. The UN Environmental Programme estimates that an area of rain forest equal to one square mile is destroyed in the world every six minutes. An area the size of Austria is cut down each year. One tree is planted for every ten that are felled. At this rate, the remaining rain forests will be gone by the year 2035.

It is easy to say, "save the rain forests." But people must eat. When people are hun-

gry, politicians find it hard to say "No!" It is much more popular to give people land— even if it is precious rain forest land.

So, people come in. They clear the land and plant crops. The crops do well for a year or two. But rain forest land is unusual. There are few nutrients and all are at the top of the soil. Before long, the rich top layer is worn away. Nothing but grass will grow. Within a few more years, the land is dead and barren.

The population of many developing nations is expected to double by the year 2020. To survive, people will plant on whatever land is available. Even where rain forests are protected by law, few countries have the money to see that protection policies are carried out. If the rain forests around the world disappear, so will the native peoples, such as the Lacandon, who live in them.

As early as the 1950s, Trudi and Franz Blom understood the problems facing the Lacandon. They bought an old building near the Lacandon rain forest. It would become their home and a center for the study of the ancient Maya and their descendants. The Lacandon Indians called Franz Blom the "jaguar." The name Blom was similar to *bolom*, the Mayan word for this animal, sacred to the Lacandones. Trudi and Franz called their home *Na Bolom* or the "house of the jaguar."

Na Bolom quickly became a center and a meeting place for friends, visitors and scholars eager to learn more about the Maya. Archaeologists stopped there on their way to the ruins of Mayan cities they were excavating. Anthropologists visited in between trips to speak with the nearby Indians whose traditions were much like those of their ancestors. Extra rooms were rented to paying guests to help support the work of the center. Each room was decorated with crafts from a different village in Chiapas and with Trudi's moving black-and-white photographs.

Trudi herself was accepted by the Lacandones in a way few outsiders ever are. She took the time to learn about their ways. She photographed them at work and play. She used her pictures to tell others about them. Today her photos are still part of touring photographic exhibits on Mexico and its people.

Gertrude Blom as an older woman. Copyright © Na Bolom.

Trudi knew that the rain forest was crucial to the survival of the Lacandones. She was also realistic about the problems of rain forest protection.

Very few people … have an idea of what the forest means, not just as beauty, but for the humanity of the world, for the diversity … and as long as the … masses cannot understand that, then the forest will go.[4]

Always practical, Trudi did what could be done. She brought in trained tree specialists. With their help, she established a nursery. Because of her efforts, between 25,000 and 30,000 seedlings are planted throughout the region each year. The young trees

27

are contributed free to people who will plant them. The money for the seedlings came from what she earned giving lectures to university students and environmental groups around the world.

Trudi Blom died at the age of 92 in December of 1993. Her love of the Lacandon people, however, lives on. Na Bolom remains a center for scholars and environmentalists concerned about the descendants of the ancient Maya and their homeland. Her tree nursery continues to provide seedlings and hope. Her photographs bear witness to the traditional Lacandon culture. And her words stand as a warning and inspiration to all:

> Let's think about the future or else we are going to be the last species left on this planet.[5]

WHAT YOU CAN DO

1. Learn more about the Lacandon Indians by reading *Heirs of the Ancient Maya: A Portrait of the Lacandon Indians* by Christine Price with photographs by Gertrude Duby Blom (New York: Charles Scribner's Sons, 1972).

2. Support efforts to purchase rain forest land around the world. One organization that does this is the Children's Rain Forest. Find out how you can help by writing to them at Box 936, Lewiston, ME 04240.

3. Learn more about rain forests and tell others. One good resource is *The Rainforest Book: How You Can Save the World's Rainforests* by Scott Lewis (Venice, CA: Living Planet Press, 1990). You can also write to The Rainforest Alliance for a free fact sheet. Their address is 65 Bleecker Street, New York, NY 10012-2420.

4. Listen to the sounds of a rainforest. One good resource is *Jungle*, an audiotape of rainforest sounds available for $12 postpaid from Nature Recordings, P.O. Box 2749, Friday Harbor, WA 98250. The sights and sounds of a rainforest can be explored in the videotape *Rain Forest* produced by the National Geographic Society (60 minutes long, 1983). Check for it at your local library.

5. Build a model of a rainforest and use it in a presentation for your class or for younger students. One good resource is *Make Your Own Rainforest* by Damian Johnston, Andrew Mitchell, Carol Watson and Gill Tomblin. It includes a three-dimensional press-out rainforest model to make (New York: Lodestar Books, 1993).

6. Support the work of Na Bolom, Av. Vicente Guerrero nr. 33, 29220 San Cristóbal de las Casas, Chiapas, Mexico. Donations may be made in care of the Richard L. Hoffman Foundation for Developing Countries, P.O. Box 490, Mars Hill, NC 28754. (Checks should be made out to the Richard L. Hoffman Foundation: Na Bolom Endowment Fund.)

Jane Goodall and her son "Grub." Copyright © Archive Photos.

Chapter Four

JANE GOODALL AND THE CHIMPS OF GOMBE

"I cannot remember a time when I did not want to go to Africa to study animals."

—*Jane Goodall*

The slender, blond woman had been walking for almost an hour. Far above her, the trees of the African rain forest shut out the sunlight. A wet mist clung to everything. Here and there, red and white flowers peeked through the dark leaves. She squatted down on the forest floor, took out a notebook and binoculars, and settled down to watch. She knew she might sit here for hours.

Without warning, a troop of redtail monkeys came scuffling overhead. Branches crackled as they scrambled from one tree to another. Almost as quickly, they were gone. With a sharp squawk, a kingfisher flew past. He too disappeared into the shadows.

Suddenly, the woman heard what she had been waiting and watching for—a troop of wild chimpanzees. For an instant, her thoughts flashed to a childhood memory. She was five years old. She and her mother were visiting relatives in the countryside. Jane had been missing for hours, and her relatives were frantic with worry.

"Jane, where have you been!" her mother asked sharply.

"Only to the henhouse," Jane had replied.

"We've been looking for you for four hours! I just finished talking with the police." Suddenly, the annoyance in her mother's voice gave way to curiosity. "What were you doing in the henhouse?" she asked.

"I was watching the hens," Jane had answered.
"For four hours?" asked her mother.
"I wanted to see how a hen laid an egg," said Jane. Instead of scolding her
daughter, Jane's mother had smiled. Now, years later, Jane was once again
waiting patiently and watching animals.

Jane Goodall was born in 1934 in Bournemouth, England. Her parents were Mortimer and Vanne Morris-Goodall. Jane was fascinated by animals from the very beginning. Even an earthworm was special to her. When she put one on the soft earth, she could see how it moved its slender body to work its way back into the ground. One of Jane's earliest playthings was a soft toy chimpanzee. It was named Jubilee after the first chimp born in the London Zoo. To this day, Jane still has that toy chimp. Jane always knew she would go to Africa one day. But how she would get there—that she did not know.

Jane's parents were divorced while she was in high school. There was no money to send her to college. Instead, Jane got a job in an office in London.

A former schoolmate of Jane's had moved with her family to Kenya. (Kenya was under the control of the British government from 1895 until 1963. A number of British citizens still lived there.) When her childhood friend invited her for a visit, Jane jumped at the chance to see a part of Africa. She quit her job in London and went back home to her mother's house in the English countryside to save money. She spent the summer living at home, working as a waitress and setting aside every penny. Finally she had enough for the trip.

Soon after her arrival in Kenya, someone suggested that she visit Dr. Louis Leakey. He was head of Kenya's National Museum of Natural History in Nairobi. He and his wife, Mary, were searching for the remains of early humans in the dusty ground of Oldevai Gorge.

Jane felt uncomfortable about contacting this famous man. After all, why should he bother to speak to her? It is not always easy to overcome shyness, but Jane did. She contacted him, and he agreed to meet her. Without realizing it, Jane had set herself on an exciting new path. It would become her life's work. Dr. Leakey offered her a job at the museum. Jane was thrilled. It meant she could stay in this strange and wonderful country she already loved.

In time, Jane went to Oldevai Gorge with Dr. Leakey and his wife. Long ago, early humans had lived and died there. Their bones were turned to rock-hard fossils with the passing of millions of years. Their stone tools lay beside them in the dry, packed earth. The work of finding the fossils was hot and tiring. Jane worked for long hours in 110-degree heat each day. Using delicate tools, she sifted through the dirt. She looked for bone fragments that fit together like jigsaw puzzle pieces. Dr. Leakey was pleased with her work. He noticed how observant she was, and how patient. Jane was fascinated by the work—even with the scorching African sun overhead.

Oddly, the discussion in the evenings was not about fossils. It was about chimpanzees. Dr. Leakey wanted to do more than piece together how early humans looked. He wanted to know how they lived. He longed to step inside their world and understand them.

Dr. Leakey had an unusual theory. He believed that by studying chimpanzees, more could be learned about what life was like for early humans. No one had ever done a long-term study of chimpanzees in the wild. When Dr. Leakey asked Jane if she would be willing to try such a study, she could hardly believe her luck. She had no formal scientific training. All she had was a love of science and the will to observe carefully and patiently. Eagerly, Jane agreed.

Before long, Dr. Leakey had arranged for the research to be funded. Jane was to travel to Gombe on the shores of Lake Tanganyika in Tanzania. Here there was a large area of land set aside as a refuge where many animals, including chimps, could be found. Then came the bad news. African officials would not

allow a young Englishwoman to work alone in such a wild area. It would be too dangerous, they said.

Jane's hopes seemed ruined. It looked as if her dream of studying the chimps would not come true. Then someone surprised her. Jane's mother agreed to go too. It meant hardship. Their camp would be simple—no running water, no electricity, with only canned food to eat. But Vanne Goodall knew how important this opportunity was to her daughter. Life would never be the same for either of them.

Each day Jane hiked into the dense African forest to watch for chimps. Wary of humans, they hid from her. Days went by without sight of a single one. Some people might have given up. Not Jane Goodall. Finally, with all her patience, Jane began to catch glimpses of the chimps now and then. This led to a new problem. She could not tell the chimps apart. At first, they all looked alike. After a time, however, she began to notice small differences. One had a bit of gray fur on his chin. Another had ragged ears. This was how she came to know them.

Jane wrote down everything she saw the chimps do, no matter how unimportant it seemed. She also gave them names. There was David Greybeard and a mother chimp Jane named Flo. Soon, Jane began to notice that the chimps had different personalities too. Some, like Flo, were well liked by the other chimps. A few were inclined to fight. Some were shy, while others were outgoing.

One day, Jane had had an especially frustrating morning. She had tramped over miles of forest without seeing a single chimp. The rainy season had begun. Her clothes were soaked. She was tired.

Suddenly, she stopped. Far ahead there was a movement in the grass. What could it be? A snake? A baboon? Quickly, she focused her binoculars. She saw a single chimpanzee. He was squatting beside a termite nest. When he turned in her direction, she recognized David Greybeard. What was he doing?

Quietly, so as not to disturb him, Jane moved closer. As she watched, the male chimp carefully pushed a long stem of grass into a termite nest in the ground. After a moment, he pulled it gently back out. Then he picked something from the end of the grass stem with his lips. He was using the stem as a tool to get at and eat the crunchy insects.

This was an important discovery. Before, it was thought that only humans used tools. Indeed, humans were defined as the only animals who made and used tools. A lot of science books would have to be rewritten because of what Jane Goodall had seen!

Over the next few months, Jane saw chimps not just using tools, but making them. They were not happy with just any old stick for reaching into a termite nest. They broke off sticks to exactly the right length and carefully stripped off the leaves. In their actions, Jane saw the beginnings of toolmaking.

Later Jane observed the chimps make and use other tools. They used leaves as napkins to wipe themselves clean. They also made sponges of chewed leaves to soak up water from a pool to drink. When Jane had observed the chimps doing something, such as chewing a leaf to make a sponge, she often tried it herself. She even sampled the things they ate such as bark, leaves, grubs and insects!

Over time, Jane observed the chimps doing things no one had ever dreamed possible. She saw them greet one another excitedly with hugs, or walk together holding hands. She also saw them fighting.

David Greybeard would never know how much he had helped Jane. Her discovery of him using a tool helped raise interest in her work. It meant she would get the money to continue her study. David Greybeard was also the first chimp to let Jane come near him. Jane had always believed that the chimps would learn to accept her one day. Because of David Greybeard, the others came to accept Jane too.

A young photographer arrived at Gombe to take pictures of the chimps. His name was Hugo Van Lawick. In time he and Jane fell in love and were married. Their son, also named Hugo, was born in 1967. His parents nicknamed him Grub. This means "bush baby" in Swahili, the language of the people who live near Gombe. Having a baby did not stop Jane from studying the chimps. Indeed, watching them gave her ideas on how to raise her own son.

During her stay at Gombe, Jane observed many chimp mothers. She saw that they seldom left their babies alone and were very affectionate toward them. Jane tried to raise her son the same way. She gave him lots of attention. And, when Grub was naughty, she did not punish him. Instead, she would turn his attention to something else.

As Grub grew older, he quickly learned to be careful in the forest. At the age of three, he visited his grandmother, Vanne Goodall, back in England. When the ball he was playing with rolled under a bush, he hit the bush with a stick. This was to be sure there were no dangerous animals hidden beneath its branches. Only when he was sure it was safe did he reach in among the leaves for his ball. Grub's life was being shaped by the unique experience of growing up in the African wilderness.

Observing animals is often lonely work. But not always. One day, as Jane sat watching the chimp David Greybeard, she noticed something. A ripe red palm nut was lying on the ground. She knew it was a tasty treat for a chimpanzee. She picked it up and held it out to him. Jane later wrote:

> He turned his head away. When I moved my hand closer he looked at it, then at me, and then he took the fruit and at the same time held my hand firmly and gently in his own. As I sat motionless he released my hand, looked down at the nut, and dropped it to the ground.[1]

Although David Greybeard apparently did not want the nut, it was as if he did not want to hurt her feelings by rejecting it. In that moment of connection with another species, Jane felt greatly rewarded.

Jane Goodall and her husband, Baron Hugo Van Lawick. Copyright © Archive Photos.

Perhaps in some small way, this experience made up for Jane's early rejection by other scientists. When she began her work, many scientists snubbed her. They did not like the way she wrote about her work. In her articles, she used the names she had given the chimps. One paper she wrote was returned to her with an icy request to refer to the chimps by number, not name. That was the proper scientific method. Jane also described the chimps she had come to know as if they had feelings. Even today, some scientists reject the idea that nonhuman animals have feelings or emotions. Years later, Jane would write:

> How naive I was. As I had not had an undergraduate science education I didn't realize that animals were not supposed to have personalities, or to think, or to feel emotions or pain … . Not knowing, I freely made use of all those forbidden terms and concepts in my initial attempt to describe, to the best of my ability, the amazing things I had observed at Gombe.[2]

That was thirty years ago. Today, things are different. Chimpanzees are now understood to have behavior patterns, intelligence and even emotions similar to our own. Things are different for Jane Goodall too. She holds a Ph.D. from Cambridge University in England. She has received many conservation awards, and she lectures at colleges around the world. Her books and articles are published in many languages. Her appearances on television shows like *20/20*, *Nightline* and *Good Morning, America* have made her famous.

Today, Jane seldom has time to observe the chimps. Her study is carried on by other scientists. Her time is divided between lecturing on chimp behavior and working to protect chimpanzees and their habitat.

Jane believes that if her work had not begun at Gombe when it did, the chimps would have lost their habitat by now. The world might never have learned about them. At that time, people living nearby wanted to farm the land where the chimps make their home. Because of Jane's work, the chimps and their habitat became famous. As a result, the question of letting people take over the land was dropped.

Even so, the area where the chimps live has shrunk over the past 30 years. The chimpanzees are living in a kind of wild prison. Their habitat is surrounded on three sides by villages and farms. The fourth side is bordered by a lake.

Jane believes that when she began her work, there may have been 10,000 chimpanzees in Tanzania. Today there are fewer than 2,500. At the turn of the century, chimps were to be found in more than two dozen African nations. Today they have disappeared in all but a few countries. Why the drop in their numbers? The chimps have lost out to the needs of the ever-growing human population. Forests are cut down to make farmland. Habitat is destroyed by mining and logging. The number of chimps is further reduced by the captive wildlife trade. Mother chimpanzees are killed so their babies can be caught and sold. Some countries have laws against this. But as long as people are willing to pay for chimpanzees from the wild, the illegal trade goes on.

Today, Jane Goodall's work takes her far from the chimps of Gombe. Protecting them and their habitat takes up most of her time. It means traveling. It means going to fundraising events since money is needed to buy land where the chimps live. It means giving lectures and interviews to educate the public. All of this is exhausting. What keeps her going? When Jane thinks of the chimps that have already lost so much of their forest home, it gives her the strength to keep on.

WHAT YOU CAN DO

1. Learn more about Jane's work by reading *My Life with Chimpanzees* by Jane Goodall (New York: Minstrel Books, 1988).

2. See what it is like to observe chimps in their native African habitat by watching the National Geographic Society's videotape *Among the Wild Chimpanzees* (59 minutes, 1987). Check for it at your local library.

3. Support the work of Jane Goodall by joining her organization for young naturalists, Roots and Shoots. In the United States, membership costs $2 per student. For more information, write to the Jane Goodall Institute, P.O. Box 599, Ridgefield, CT 06877.

Barbara Kerr (right) and her sister Gwen sit on the steps of their home in North Carolina in 1927. Copyright © Barbara Kerr.

Chapter Five

BARBARA KERR COOKS WITH SUN POWER

"Experiencing the changes in life over the years has meant more to me than simple aging. It has meant watching the landscape and the world become more tame, drab, and developed. Human life and wildlife are both losing their world."

—*Barbara Kerr*

It is sometime in the future. A girl is walking up the path that leads to her family's house. The house is built into the side of a hill. On the roof, four large solar panels are tilted to receive the sun's rays. The panels provide energy for the family's appliances. Solar collectors heat their hot water. Inside the house, the air is cool even though it is warm and sunny outdoors. In the kitchen, the girl's father is using a solar dehydrator to dry some of the vegetables from their garden. That way they can be stored for use later. He tosses unwanted bits of vegetable into a bin in which live worms are busy breaking down food scraps into soil. One of the girl's chores is sprinkling the broken-down soil or compost outside in their garden. Next to the compost bin are three other bins. These are for recyclables—since nearly everything today comes in recyclable packages and there is very little waste.

"Use it up, wear it out, make it do, or do without" is a saying that might have applied to Barbara Kerr's childhood. Except for one thing. Her family did not do without. They did not have to. Barbara's father, an amateur inventor, saw to that.

Barbara Prosser Kerr, creator of the Kerr-Cole Solar Box Cooker, was born in 1925.

She grew up in the Great Smoky Mountains in North Carolina. In Barbara's part of the country many things were handmade. "The ability to figure out ways to do things you needed was highly prized," explains Barbara. "We just did not buy things lightly. I learned to think about what I needed, what would do that kind of a job, and how I could put it together so it would work."[1]

Barbara has always had an inventive mind. She inherited that from her father. When Barbara was a child, she helped her father as he created useful things for their family. In addition to their home in town, they had a cabin in the mountains that they used on weekends. The cabin had no running water. Barbara's father decided to do something about that.

> He placed a dark 55-gallon drum on a bright metal roof and ran a long hose from the spring near the top of the mountain behind the cabin. He ran a pipe into the kitchen for the sink. And he set up a wooden grate behind the house with a showerhead hanging out from the edge of the roof. One of my early morning chores was to go out behind the cabin and turn the spigot that allowed the ice-cold mountain water to flow into the drum until it overflowed and then I had to shut it off. I would sit on the bank and listen to the birds while waiting for the barrel to fill. It was peaceful ... While the water was ice cold at 9 A.M., by 11 it was getting warm enough to wash dishes.[2]

There were no people around, so the outdoor shower had no curtain. Barbara showered looking up at the trees and the sky. She found that if she showered at one or even two o'clock, the water was quite warm, or even hot. But one bright, sunny day she waited until three o'clock to shower. "The water was so hot I danced out yelling!" recalls Barbara. She found that her skin had turned red from the heat of the water. "Once you have been almost blistered from solar-heated water, you can never wonder if solar energy will work!"[3] Barbara would eventually begin to wonder what else solar energy could do.

Barbara grew up feeling close to nature. When she was young, she recalls, the pace of life was slower than it is for most Americans today. The forests "were so thick you had to push your way along moist, green tunnels ... always accompanied by birds, lizards, and little things that scuttled away with soft noises .... I was a child when telephones had four numbers and the operator knew you personally," she recalls, "—long before there were painted lines on roads, when you shopped by standing at the counter and asking the clerk for each item on your list, well before supermarkets .... We had cars, but ice and some groceries were delivered to our neighborhood by horse-drawn wagon."[4]

Barbara's father was a strong influence on her. "My father told me that if I could not take care of a tool or could not repair something I had, I did not really own it. It would soon be broken and gone. It was really only yours if you could make your own tool or whatnot to do the job you needed. I learned to think that way and make a lot of what I needed.[5]

In time, Barbara grew up and left home. She studied nursing at Galinger Hospital, now the Capital City School of Nursing in

Washington, D.C. She married in 1950, and her daughter Diana was born in 1954. Five years later, while working as a head nurse at Bronx Municipal Hospital, Barbara contracted tuberculosis. Her recovery was long and painful. Nursing proved too physically strenuous and she sought other work.

Barbara decided to go into social work. She earned a master's degree in the subject from the University of Pennsylvania. But she continued to have respiratory problems. Soon after graduating, she learned that the pollution in Philadelphia was too severe for her. She moved to Tempe, Arizona, where she worked for many years as an emergency room social worker. Her patients were car accident victims, rape victims and others who had undergone severe trauma. It was a stressful job. It was at this point in her life that she realized she needed a hobby to help relieve the stress of her job. The answer turned out to be solar cooking.

Barbara had grown up with an appreciation for the natural world. Now she saw the environment changing, as more and more resources were used up. She wanted to find ways to save natural resources. She was also interested in making the lives of women easier. "Where I was raised," she says, "the mountain women did most of the labor around the house and garden. They were often tired and poorly fed. Sadly, this is the situation with many women around the world."[6]

Barbara knew how to cook. She also knew the power of solar energy, having had the experience of burning herself on solar-heated water in her childhood home. She knew that the sun would provide even more energy in Arizona where she now lived. Here the sun shines most days of the year. Before she knew it, she had made a solar box cooker.

A solar box cooker is any kind of box that uses the heat of the sun to cook. How does it work? The inside of a box is heated by sunlight. A piece of glass is put in the lid of the box to allow sunlight in. Part of the inside of the box is painted black because a dark surface makes for greater heat. The box is insulated, that is, padded with newspapers, so the heat stays inside. Usually a reflector is attached to the box in some way to send extra sunlight through the glass and into the box. A box like this can cook at fairly high temperatures. It may take a little longer, but the food does not dry out and does not need to be stirred.

Why does it work? There are three solar energy laws involved. (1) Sunlight passes through a piece of glass easily, but heat does not, so heat can be trapped. (2) When sunlight strikes a dark surface (like the inside of the box painted black) it changes to heat. (3) When light falls on a shiny surface (a reflector), it reflects or bounces off and can be pointed or sent in a certain direction.

Eco-Women

The first solar box cooker was actually made a long time ago. A Swiss naturalist named Horace de Saussure experimented with box cookers that used the sun's heat as early as 1767.

After a number of tries with different kinds of cookers, Barbara tried putting one small box inside a larger one. That turned out to be the secret. Her first cooker reached a temperature of 240 degrees. (It takes 212 degrees to boil water.) After more improvements, she developed one that would reach 300 degrees—hot enough to boil, roast and bake. She would put the food into the box early in the day and leave it untended for hours. By mealtime, a hearty lunch or dinner would be ready with almost no effort.

In the mid-1970s, a number of people around the world were experimenting with solar box cookers. Most of these were made of wood or metal. Not knowing that it "should" be made of these materials, Barbara made her cooker out of cardboard boxes, glass and tape. Before long, different cookers of all shapes and sizes starting sprouting up in her backyard. Her neighbor, Sherry Cole, loved it! She offered lots of great suggestions. Where Barbara was the dreamer, Sherry was practical. Sherry also took on the job of answering letters and making personal contacts to let people know about the new invention. Without Sherry's help, the solar box cooker "could have come and gone,"[7] says Barbara. Because of Sherry's efforts, the cooker was fea-tured in news articles and on the radio. In time, other people became interested in Barbara's unusual "garden" of backyard solar cookers as well.

Barbara smiles when she recalls how she was told to drop her "box" approach to solar cooking altogether. The design was all wrong, one university student told her. It could not possibly work. He "proved" his point by showing her a mathematical table in a text-book. Unfortunately, says Barbara, as he spoke, he was seated next to "a solar box that was quietly and cheerfully cooking a large

Barbara Kerr's invention means a lot to people in places like Mali where there is plenty of sunshine. It means that food can be cooked without cutting trees for firewood. Copyright © Solar Cookers International.

pot of beans."[8] Maybe he thought the solar cooker could not work because it appeared to be made out of junk—a couple of old boxes, some tape and a piece of glass. It goes to show that you can't go by looks alone!

"The basic solar box cooker … is so simple," says Barbara, "people often think, 'So, what's the big deal? Anybody could make one of those.' That is music to my ears! The big deal is that these designs work! They cook! And they cook on free, abundant sunshine."[9]

Dr. Robert Metcalf, a professor at California State University in Sacramento, was excited by the simplicity of Barbara's cooker. He knew it could be used in developing nations. He was sure it would save lives.

What do you do when you want a glass of water? You turn on the faucet, fill your glass and drink. Nothing special, right? Wrong! In many parts of the world, water must be hauled from a town faucet, pump or water hole. Carrying water is hard work. Also, in some places, the water is dirty. It may have sand or grit in it. Dirty water can also carry a germ that makes people very sick. Sometimes people die from drinking the dirty water. So, having fresh, clean water at the turn of a faucet is pretty special after all.

Making sure that water is clean for drinking is important. In many developing countries, people need to boil water before drinking it—even if the water comes out of a tap. Boiling kills the germ that can make people sick. That sounds easy enough. But in places like Africa and India, cooking is usually not done on a stove. It is done over an open fire. Also, in many places such as these, trees have

been cut down in large numbers. They may have been cut to provide land for farming. Or, they may have been cut to sell for wood products made and sold in other countries like the United States. Because the trees have been cut down, often there is not much wood for the people to use in building cooking fires. What wood there is may be used for cooking food, instead of boiling water. Not everyone knows how important it is to boil drinking water.

The governments of developing nations are working hard to educate people about the need to boil water before drinking it. But what good does it do to tell people they need to boil the water, if they have no firewood to boil it with? Until recently, there was no answer.

With Robert Metcalf's help, an organization was formed to help provide the Kerr-Cole Solar EcoCookers to people in developing nations. Today, Solar Cookers International (SCI) brings solar cookers to thousands of people around the world. The cookers are being used in Zimbabwe, Sudan, Ecuador, Guatemala, Bolivia, Chile, Mexico and India. SCI was represented at the Earth Summit in Rio de Janeiro in 1992. Even so, changing people's habits takes a long time.

Barbara is pleased that her solar box cooker is being put to such good use. But it is really only one part of a much larger project for her. Barbara has gone on to develop other devices for Earth-friendly living. Today, she lives in an unusual house. It is both a home and a center for helping people develop an environmentally friendly lifestyle. The Sustainable Living Center, where Barbara lives, is unique because it makes so few demands on the Earth's resources. People come from many different places to see the center and learn from Barbara.

Barbara's home involves a special combination of high-tech solutions and common sense. For instance, solar collectors heat the water. Solar (photovoltaic) panels make the electricity for running lights and appliances. On the other hand, Barbara's "solar" clothes dryer is a clothesline in the sun. "Hanging clothes in the sun makes them smell wonderful!" smiles Barbara.[10] Her air conditioning system is quite simple. Her home is built into the side of a hill, keeping it cool in summer and also reducing heat loss in winter.

Barbara grows much of her own food in her garden. She composts vegetable garbage and recycles other trash. She has a special system so that gray water (used water) may be used again for jobs, like scrubbing the floor, that do not require clean water.

Solar cooking remains an important part of Barbara Kerr's environment-friendly household. It "ties all my caring together,"[11] she says. At age 70, she continues to design devices that will improve the Sustainable Living Center. She is proud that her home was on the Real Goods National Tour of Independent Homes for the past three years in a row.

Can one person make a difference for the Earth? With her invention of the Kerr-Cole Solar EcoCooker and her Sustainable Living Center, Barbara Kerr answers, "Yes!"

WHAT YOU CAN DO

1. Barbara has a suggestion for you and your family. With your parents' input, choose one of these three resources to work on saving at your home: fuel for heating the home, water or electricity. Ask your parents for the utility bills for that resource for the past three years. If these are not available, try contacting the utility company. In some places, utility companies will supply past bills. Graph the units of consumption (amounts of the resource you used) for the resource you chose. (Basing your graph on units of consumption, rather than on money, will keep the graph steady in spite of price changes.) Then make a game out of saving. Figure out what an average bill should be. If a bill comes in under that amount, the extra can go to a special fund—for family outings or entertainment. It's a great way to cooperate, practice saving resources and have a good time.

2. Build your own solar box cooker. For plans, send a check in the amount of $2.85 to Kerr Enterprises, P.O. Box 27417, Tempe, AZ 85285. More complex solar cooker plans are also available. Write for more information.

3. Learn more about alternative energy sources and the importance of saving energy. One good resource is *The Kids' Environment Book: What's Awry and Why* by Anne Pedersen (Santa Fe, NM: John Muir Publications, 1991).

4. Learn more about solar energy in particular. One good resource is *Energy from the Sun* by Jan Burgess (Lexington, MA: Grolier Educational Corporation, 1988). Or, try some of the solar activities in *Sunpower Experiments: Solar Energy Explained* by Maggie Spooner (New York: Sterling Publishing, 1981).

5. Support the work of Solar Cookers International (SCI) at 1724 Eleventh Street, Sacramento, CA 95814. Write for their free brochure *Sunshine—Free Cooking Power*.

Barbara Kerr and Robert Metcalf of Solar Cookers International. Copyright © Solar Cookers International.

As a girl, Katy Payne was fascinated by the world of nature. She enjoyed hiking and observing the animals in and around her home. Copyright © Katharine Payne.

Chapter Six
LISTENING TO ELEPHANTS WITH KATHARINE PAYNE

"People use oil that they get from whales and ivory that they get from elephants. These things are worth a great deal of money. But they cost more than money—they cost life itself. I think that is too great a price to pay for oil and ivory, so I try to help people understand what the world is losing."

—*Katharine Payne*

The hot African sun beats down on the gray jeep. A fair-skinned woman sits in the back of the vehicle. A tape recorder lies on the seat beside her. Microphones dangle out the window. She sits as still and quiet as possible as a herd of elephants steps powerfully toward the jeep. Before long, they are all around her. Large gray mother elephants; small babies with a rusty fuzz of hair on their heads; wrinkled elderly aunts. … One wise old grandmother elephant—the mother of all—leads them. Suddenly, the elephants too are still. Everyone from the largest to the smallest stands frozen, motionless, with stiffened ears held a little higher than usual. They are listening to a world and a depth of sound which we humans cannot hear.

Katy Payne is a scientist in the field of bioacoustics. *Bio* means "life" and *acoustics* means "sound." Katy studies the sounds that wild animals make and what those sounds communicate. Her effort to understand whalesong has helped whales. People became more interested in protecting whales after they heard the beautiful, haunting sounds that whales make. Now that Katy's focus has turned to elephants, she hopes her work may have a similar effect. African elephants are endangered. Katy believes that the public can learn to appreciate these majestic animals and choose to protect them.

Katy Boynton Payne was born in Ithaca, New York, in 1937—a mile from where she lives today. She grew up on an old-fashioned farm. It was made up of fields, orchards, gardens and a stream with waterfalls. Her father was an apple grower and a professor at nearby Cornell University. Her mother loved books and music. Her grandfather was a famous wildlife artist named Louis Agassiz Fuertes. Growing up with her were a brother, Louis, four years older; and a sister, Mia, seven years younger than she.

As a child, Katy liked to go exploring. Ithaca has many rocky gorges where she went hiking every chance she got. And, like her famous grandfather, Katy loved to watch wild animals. She also enjoyed watching and helping out with the animals on the farm: chickens, sheep, pigs, cows, dogs, cats and a pony.

In 1954 Katy went to Cornell University where she majored in music. While singing in a performance of Bach's *St. Matthew Passion*, Katy met Roger Payne. He was playing the cello in the performance and was a graduate student in biology at Cornell. They were married in 1960. One year later,

their first child, John, was born. Over the next three years, Holly, Laura and Sam arrived as well. Roger earned his degree and began working as a biology teacher at Tufts University in Boston, Massachusetts. Katy was busy as a mother and homemaker.

In 1966, the Paynes took a trip to Bermuda to see whales in the company of a Navy engineer named Frank Watlington. Frank's job was to listen to the sounds picked up by a collection of hydrophones—microphones that went down far into the sea. While out on his ship, he and the Paynes observed humpback whales together, and Frank decided to share a secret. While listening for noise of Navy ships and explosions, he had been recording an extraordinary collection of sounds made by whales! He took the couple into an office deep down in the ship and let them listen to a recording of whales' voices.

Frank had told only a few trusted friends about his discovery. He was afraid that whalers would use the sounds to find and hunt whales. But he trusted Roger and Katy to keep his secret, and gave them his collection of tapes to study.

As he listened to the wonderful tapes over and over again, Roger Payne noticed that the sounds were organized in long complicated patterns

that repeated every few minutes. In fact, the whales were singing songs, just as birds do, but the whale songs were much longer and more complicated. Katy then realized that whale songs change over time, with all the whales in a population keeping up with the latest version. This discovery gave the Paynes the chance to keep on studying humpback whales for many years. They studied whales near Bermuda and also near Hawaii, where the whales sing a different but also ever-changing song.

Eventually, the family started spending much time on the remote Patagonian coastline of Argentina. Here, they studied right whales. These whales lived so close to shore that by looking over the edge of a cliff the Paynes could identify the different whales and see what they were doing. These expeditions sometimes lasted for years. The Payne children missed some ordinary schooling. But they were living in the presence of whales and seals, of sea elephants, gigantic albatrosses and eagles. Best of all, they were developing a sense of wonder. All of the children are now grown up. They agree that the Patagonia years were among the best in their lives.

Science often takes a great deal of patience. Fortunately, Katy Payne is a patient person—and hard-working. She listened to countless hours of whalesong. She would listen over and over to the same tape

until she could pick out the different voices within a group of singing whales. Her music background helped her find patterns in the songs. She discovered that songs of certain years contained rhymes. She guessed that the rhymes helped the whales remember the current version of the song as it changed through time.

Katy was still studying whale songs in 1984 when she made a lucky discovery that changed the course of her life. Following a

Katy Payne's efforts to study the songs made by humpback whales have helped inspire people to want to protect more whales. Copyright © Robin Hunter/U.S. Fish and Wildlife Service.

whale conference that had taken her to the west coast, she made a visit to the Metro Washington Zoo in Portland, Oregon. There she spent a week in the elephant enclosure watching three mother elephants with new babies. While she was there, she noticed something. Every now and then she felt a throbbing or fluttering in the air near the elephants. She recalled, years before, the sounds of the deepest organ pipes when she had been singing the *St. Matthew Passion* in the chapel choir.

> My place was in front of the organ pipes that made the very deepest, lowest notes. When the organist played these notes, the air around me would throb and flutter. The lower down the notes went, the less I could hear them, and yet I could still feel the air throbbing. I was reaching the bottom of what human ears can hear.[1]

In the zoo, Katy experienced the same feeling of air throbbing all around her. Could it be that the elephants were making deep low sounds—so low that humans could not hear? Before long, Katy returned to the zoo with two old friends. Using special equipment to record sounds below the range of human hearing, they made tape recordings of the elephants. Katy's guess was correct. She and her friends discovered that elephants use powerful, low sounds—called infrasound—to communicate across long distances.

Katy was invited to go to Africa. Scientists Cynthia Moss and Joyce Poole were already there studying elephants in the wild. They were working in a place called Amboseli in Kenya, East Africa. It was at the foot of the great mountain Kilimanjaro.

Thousands of years ago, a lake dried up in what is now Amboseli. It left behind a barren, dusty land. (The name Amboseli means "salty dust" in the language of the people who live nearby.) Around where the lake dried up, however, there remained a swamp where water could always be found. Elephants and other animals came here to drink.

Cynthia and Joyce had studied the elephants from inside a truck. The truck stayed near the elephants day after day. Sitting inside the truck hour after hour was not always easy. But once the elephants were used to the truck, the researchers could move with the herd and not frighten the elephants they were watching. In time, the elephants seemed not even to notice the people watching them.

Katy joined the research team. From inside the truck, she and Joyce wrote down which elephants they could see, and what they were doing. Meanwhile, Katy also made tape recordings of the elephants

communicating. The work was tiring, but it was also fascinating.

> It is amazing how much you can learn about animals if you watch for a long time without disturbing them. They do odd things, which at first you don't understand. Then gradually your mind opens to what it would be like to have different eyes, different ears, and different taste; different needs, different fears, and different knowledge from ours.[2]

Katy learned that female elephants spend their whole lives together in groups. Within these family groups, they take care of each other and their babies. She learned that male elephants over the age of fourteen generally do not live with their families. And, she learned about matriarchs.

A group of female elephants is led by a matriarch or an older female—a grandmother. She may be 50 or more years old. She knows much that younger elephants may not yet know. She can guide her family along hundreds of paths. She alone can show them where to find water when all else is dry. And it is she who knows the scents of hundreds of other animals—friendly ones and dangerous ones.

Katy and Joyce watched the elephants day after day. The elephants made some sounds that they could just barely hear—and many others that were "heard" only by the recording equipment.

> Sometimes we heard low calls that sounded like purring or rumbling. Sometimes we partly heard and partly felt an elephant call. ... Some of the calls ... were made by the elephants we were watching,

but others were made by elephants that were far away. For infrasound is special in another way, too: it travels farther than the sounds that we hear. It travels so well that elephants can hear each other's low calls even when they are miles apart."[3]

As Katy points out, "elephants can be joined by their deep voices even when they are separated by a forest."[4]

Why might elephants need to communicate over long distances? Katy found that there was a good reason for this. It takes a lot of food to keep an elephant, let alone a family of elephants, going. By communicating over long distances, two elephant families can stay in touch in case of danger, yet not compete for food. Rowan Martin, a scientist in Zimbabwe, had already tracked

Katy Payne is a strong believer in the importance of protecting wild places and the animals that live there. Copyright © Katharine Payne.

elephants with radio collars for years. He had found that, though separated by miles, elephant families seemed to move in the same direction for days at a time. But no one knew how they did it. Now it appears that infrasound is the answer.

Today, Katy's and Roger's four grown-up children are all working on conservation projects. They are studying fish, shorebirds, whales and forests. Their interest is a gift to them from the wild animals they lived with and the wild places they lived in as children. In return, they are giving their own gift to the wild world as they fight for its future.

Their mother is also a fighter in the struggle to protect wild places and the animals who live there. As Katy Payne writes in her book *Elephants Calling*, she has a dream. Katy hopes that:

> … a day will come when people will value wild animals not for money but for who they are and what we can learn from them. If we learn to listen as often and as well as elephants do, it is possible that listening will keep the world safe. Safe for us in our cities and villages and farms; and the great-voiced animals in the oceans and forests and plains.[5]

WHAT YOU CAN DO

1. Learn more about the work of Katharine Payne. Share the picturebook *Elephants Calling* by Katharine Payne (New York: Crown, 1992) with younger students.

2. Don't buy ivory. Keep in mind that imitation ivory may be mistaken for the real thing.

3. Learn more about elephants, their families and how they live. One good resource is by Cynthia Moss, the researcher who began the elephant study that Joyce Poole, and later Katy Payne, joined. You will enjoy reading portions of *Echo of the Elephants: The Story of an Elephant Family* by Cynthia Moss and Martyn Colbeck (New York: William Morrow and Co., 1992).

4. Learn more about the ways in which animals communicate by reading *Signs of the Apes, Songs of the Whales: Adventures in Human-Animal Communication* by George and Linda Harrar (New York: Simon & Schuster, 1989).

5. Support the work of The Humane Society of the United States (HSUS) which works to protect whales, elephants and other animals. For a free guide on how to start your own animal and environmental protection club, write to them at 2100 L Street NW, Washington, D.C. 20037. Ask for the Student Action Guide available from the Youth Education Division.

Mardy with her brother Franklin in Alaska in 1906. Copyright © Mardy Murie.

Chapter Seven
MARGARET MURIE'S PASSION
FOR WILDERNESS

"Every citizen has a responsibility toward this planet. I'm counting on the new generation coming up. I have to believe in their spirit as those who came before me believed in mine."
—*Margaret Murie*

Even in the year 1911, Seattle was a bustling seaport. The boats for Alaska always sailed at nine o'clock in the evening so the wharf was brightly lighted and crowded with passengers, crew members and people saying goodbye. Seeing off a friend or relative bound for Alaska was a special occasion in those days. You might not see the person again for months or even years. The annual winter freeze made boat travel impossible for six months out of the year.

Shouting "gangway!" burly stevedores wove in and out through the crowd with their handcarts piled high. Crates and boxes were everywhere. Some people were shouting. Others were laughing or crying. The noises of churning engines, hissing steam and clanging ship's bells mingled with salty sea air, the acrid odor of black tar and the musty scent of hemp rope. In the midst of all this bustle, few people noticed a little girl in a bright red coat and hat. Eagerly, she clutched her many colorfully wrapped going-away presents and watched all the excitement. A uniformed man helped her up the narrow gangplank and she took her place beside her mother at the rail of the huge white ship bound for the North. Before long, the steamer Jefferson *pulled slowly out from the pier and moved into the cool, black, windy bay. Her wilderness adventure had begun!*

Nine-year-old Margaret, better known as "Mardy," loved the excitement of life aboard a passenger ship. It was great fun playing hide-and-seek or exploring the ship with the other youngsters. After a morning of racing about on deck, she enjoyed afternoons resting in the velvet-cushioned lounge while her mother sewed and chatted with other ladies. At night, she liked falling asleep to the soft, steady throb of the ship's engines and the gentle hiss of water along its sides. Best of all, there was no school! Instead of sitting in a classroom or doing homework, she got to watch the beautiful wooded landscape and its occasional frontier settlements glide by. Every day brought new sights to enjoy. She loved the green forests and brown hills and rustic canyons. She could not know that one day, this majestic Alaskan wilderness would be in danger of being lost forever—or that she would play an important part in helping to preserve it.

Mardy Murie was born Margaret Elizabeth Thomas in Seattle, Washington, in 1902. Her parents divorced while she was still a baby. Her mother soon married a lawyer named Louis Gillette.

When Mardy was nine, her stepfather was appointed assistant to the U.S. District Attorney in the Alaska Territory. It meant a big change for the family. Much of Alaska was untouched wilderness. It would not even become a state for many years to come.

The United States had purchased Alaska from Russia less than 50 years earlier. Larger than Texas, California and Montana all put together, Alaska lived up to its Eskimo name—"Great Land." It was a land of glaciers, huge mountains, active volcanoes, dense forests and treeless tundra. It was home to the Eskimo or Inuit Indians. It was habitat for bears, wolves, elk, caribou, moose, beavers, seals and arctic hares. For some years after the United States purchased the land, little changed there. Native Americans and wild animals came and went as they had done for generations. Then something happened that changed the Far North forever.

In the late 1800s gold was discovered near the frontier settlements of Juneau and Nome. Before long, thousands traveled to Alaska hoping to strike it rich. Many of those who did not discover gold found they could make a living selling supplies to others. In time, more and more small towns and settlements were established. By 1911, there was a real need for law and order in this vast frontier—and that is why Mardy's stepfather was appointed to his post. Louis Gillette went on ahead of his family, traveling to what would become their new home in Fairbanks. This bustling frontier town in the center of Alaska would represent a very different way of life from what they had known. When Mardy arrived with her mother, however, she saw it all as part of a great wilderness adventure.

Mardy and her family lived in a sturdy, four-room log house. A woodshed and

Mardy raced up and down the streets, running errands for her mother on a little sled pulled by her dog Major. Soon after arriving in Fairbanks, a family friend had given her this beautiful, sweet-tempered husky who became her constant companion.

From the age of nine until she was seventeen, Mardy attended school in Fairbanks. Upon graduating from high school, she decided to go to Reed College in Portland, Oregon, to become a teacher. Two years later, she changed her mind and returned home

outhouse were attached to it. In winter, the temperature went down to anywhere from minus 20 to minus 50. On the coldest days, Mardy had to remember not to take hold of the kitchen doorknob with a wet hand; otherwise she would freeze to it and "burn" her hand. There was a telephone and electricity, but no hot and cold running water. The water from the hand pump in the kitchen was so brown and rusty that the family had its water delivered. Each day, Fred the Waterman filled up a huge barrel just inside the kitchen door and delivered extra on wash days.

Even in 1911, Fairbanks was a sizable town. Although many people had come prospecting, plenty had stayed to do business. Most of the buildings were two stories. There were stores selling groceries, dry goods and hardware. There were restaurants, bakeries and laundries. There were saloons and boarding houses in the disreputable red-light district. In an age before radio or television, Fairbanks boasted two newspapers.

Mardy at the age of thirteen in Fairbanks, Alaska. Copyright © Mardy Murie.

to Fairbanks. At the home of a friend, she met a young naturalist—"a slim blond Norwegian with the bluest eyes."[1] His name was Olaus Murie. He was on his way north to study caribou for the U.S. Biological Survey. In those days, large portions of Alaska still remained uncharted. The behavior of many animals that lived in these remote areas was largely unknown. Olaus's job was to observe and record information about the caribou so that scientists could better understand the place of these animals in the Alaskan ecosystem.

A few days later, Mardy and Olaus took a boat ride with friends. Mardy learned a little of what it meant to be a naturalist. She recalls:

> … we heard a great horned owl hoot far off in the forest. Olaus answered him. Again the owl spoke, a bit closer this time. Olaus hooted again, and so it went, until suddenly out of nowhere the dark soft shape floated into a treetop right above us on the riverbank and sat silhouetted against the golden sky.[2]

To "call in" a wild animal seemed like magic to Mardy. Later that evening Olaus drew a picture of the bird for her. After

this she regarded him as an artist as well. Actually, his skills were those of a naturalist and scientist—identifying and imitating the calls of wild creatures, sketching, observing and taking detailed notes with great patience.

Although Mardy was fond of her new friend, she was determined to finish her education. She traveled to Boston to attend Simmons College, but saw Olaus again when she returned home the following year. Over the following months, their friendship deepened. Although they disliked the idea of separation, they knew that Olaus would have to return to Washington, D.C., to report his findings on the caribou and receive new orders. Mardy, on the other hand, would have to stay. She had decided to complete her college degree at the newly established University of Alaska in Fairbanks.

Before long, Olaus returned and by the summer of 1924, the couple was engaged. The Biological Survey was sending Olaus to the Yukon to study waterfowl. Mardy and Olaus decided to get married at Anvik, a remote settlement on the Yukon River. From there, Olaus would continue his study with Mardy at his side. Her family and friends were amused at her packing camping gear rather than the fancy dresses expected of most young brides on their honeymoon.

Some friends who knew Olaus Murie's work thought that the marriage would not last. They did not know that Mardy Murie was a spunky young woman who had a deep abiding love for the wilderness as well as for the man she had married. She quickly began helping Olaus with his work. He, in turn, opened her "mind and heart to the little-known teeming, rich life going on in the trees and streams, in the mossy tundra, and in the grassy sloughs."[3] Mardy was learning to observe, appreciate and identify birds and other wild animals. She was learning how different animals fit into their ecosystems to form the great chain of life.

By the time Olaus received his next assignment, Mardy was expecting their first child. She went to stay with her parents while he spent half a year studying brown bears on the Alaska Peninsula. The separation was painful.

When Olaus returned, the couple made a big decision. Rather than have the family separated, they would take their children wherever Olaus's field work took him. In all, they had three children: Martin, Joanne and Donald. Imagine growing up in the wilderness, making your toys from the natural objects you found, playing among the trees, looking at real wild animals instead of animal pictures in books. Some people disapproved, saying that the wilderness was no place for kids. But the Murie children thrived on it.

In 1927, the Muries settled in Jackson Hole, Wyoming. It was here that the largest elk population in North America was to be found. The trouble was that the elk were dying. The Biological Survey assigned Olaus to study the problem. In time, he came to a troubling conclusion. The elk were dying because of cattle ranching. Ranching had claimed much of the elks' habitat. The elk were forced to move to areas where there were less of the foods they needed. Also, the elks' natural predators had been virtually wiped out, upsetting the balance of nature.

Caribou are among the many animals whose lives have been disrupted by the Alaska Pipeline. Copyright © U.S. Fish and Wildlife Service.

Mardy and Olaus Murie fought long and hard for establishment of the Arctic National Wildlife Refuge. Copyright © Alaska Division of Tourism.

Olaus recommended that the National Elk Refuge be enlarged to ensure the survival of the elk. His recommendation was not popular either with the government or local ranchers. In time, Olaus would leave his government work and devote himself full time to the effort to preserve wilderness.

In the mid-1930s, the Muries joined the Wilderness Society, an environmental group fighting to protect wilderness areas. In 1946, with Mardy's support, Olaus agreed to serve as the group's director. It was a big change. For years, the Muries had been a part of the wild areas they loved. Now, they took on a

Together, Mardy Murie and her husband, Olaus, devoted their lives to wilderness protection. Copyright © Phyllis Stevie, courtesy *The Living Wilderness*.

different challenge. Olaus and Mardy traveled around the country for the Wilderness Society. They gave lectures, testified at government hearings, lobbied for new laws and raised public awareness. Whenever a park or wildlife refuge was threatened by development, the Muries fought to save it. Although she called herself Olaus's secretary, Mardy was an equal partner, sharing in the work that had become their way of life.

Together they helped save Echo Park from being flooded. Part of Dinosaur National Monument, the area included rare dinosaur fossils and more than 100 miles of beautiful canyons. The government wanted to build a dam to supply electricity to nearby homes and businesses. The dam, however, would have left Echo Park under water.

A similar dam would have flooded the Cloud Peak Primitive Area in Wyoming. The Muries fought against it. They believed that wilderness had a right to exist for its own sake. In the end, they won the battle to save Cloud Peak. They won other battles throughout the West as well, including San Gorgonio in California, Selway-Bitterroot in Idaho and Montana and Three Sisters in Oregon. They encouraged preservation of the Cascades and helped stop the Rampart Dam on the Yukon River in Alaska—the same river that Mardy had traveled by steamship as a young girl.

Olaus and Margaret also wrote about their experiences. Olaus published the results of his elk research in *The Elk of North America* in 1951. He also completed *A Field Guide to Animal Tracks*. Published in 1954, it remains to this day a standard reference guide for

naturalists. For years, Mardy had kept a diary of their life in the wilderness. She used it as the basis for a book about their early years together titled *Two in the Far North*, published in 1962.

In the mid-1950s, the Muries turned their efforts to Alaska—a land they loved and understood better than most people did. The Muries started a campaign to have a national wildlife refuge created in Alaska. The Arctic National Wildlife Refuge would cover nine million acres. It would protect the habitat of the caribou that they had followed on their honeymoon. It would protect land needed by moose, wolves, bears, foxes and countless species of birds.

The couple set out by leading an expedition to the Brooks Range to gather information. For the next eight years they attended countless hearings, made speeches, wrote articles and answered letters. It was a struggle. During it all, Olaus was fighting his own personal battle as well. He was seriously ill with cancer. He lived to hear that the Arctic National Wildlife Refuge would become a reality. He died in 1963. Mardy and Olaus

had shared a wilderness life for many years. Mardy knew that it would be painful going on alone. But she was determined to continue the work that they had shared.

One year later, Mardy attended the signing of the Wilderness Act by President Lyndon Johnson, permanently placing the area under government protection. In 1966, Mardy published her second book, *Wapiti Wilderness*. (Wapiti is an Indian word for "elk.") She and Olaus had worked on this together for some years. It portrayed their family's life in Wyoming where Olaus had gone to complete his research on elk populations.

In 1968, environmentalists would face their greatest challenge in Alaska. A huge oil deposit was discovered in the Brooks Range where Olaus had first gone to study caribou. The Alaska Pipeline was put through in 1973. It stretched across 800 miles, ending in the now famous town of Valdez—the scene of one of the most disastrous offshore oil spills ever.

In 1975, Mardy was asked to be a consultant to the National Park Service. She spent weeks visiting wilderness areas in Alaska to determine if they were worthy of protection under the National Park System. Not surprisingly, she concluded that they were. Mardy worked hard for passage of the Alaska Lands Act. It would protect more than 100 million acres of land. That sounds like a lot. But Mardy knew that, in comparison to what had already been lost, it was not nearly enough. In time, the bill passed, ensuring the protection of countless wild animals and their habitats.

Mardy had worked long and hard to protect the wild areas she loved. In 1980, her efforts were rewarded with the Audubon Medal, one of the most highly regarded environmental awards. The following year, she became the first woman to receive the Sierra Club's prestigious John Muir Award. In 1986, the Wilderness Society presented her with its own Robert Marshall Conservation Award. Her greatest reward for her efforts, however, was in knowing that through her work countless wild places and their animals would receive greater protection.

At age 94, Mardy Murie is still concerned about the environment. Her log cabin in Moose, Wyoming, remains a gathering place for environmentalists. She has wild animal visitors on occasion as well, living in an area where bears, moose, deer and other animals make their home.

Her message for young people? "You have to reach out and get acquainted with people who think likewise and are also kind of groping for a hand to hold onto. I think that kind of thing can happen. People can pick up and take off one step at a time and make a difference."[4] Making a difference is something Mardy Murie knows all about.

WHAT YOU CAN DO

1. Learn more about Mardy's life and work by reading *Margaret Murie: A Wilderness Life* by Jennifer Bryant (New York: Twenty-First Century Books, 1993).

2. Start a journal of your own observations of wild animals and their habitats. Good resources on how to begin keeping a nature journal are *Nature All Year Long* by Clare Walker Leslie (New York: Greenwillow Books, 1991) and *Drawing From Nature* by Jim Arnosky (New York: Lothrop, Lee and Shepard Books, 1982).

3. Support the work of the Wilderness Society, 900 17th Street NW, Washington, D.C. 20006-2596.

Through the Green Belt Movement, the organization that she began, Wangari Maathai is helping to bring about the planting of trees and empowerment of women in Kenya. Copyright © Goldman Environmental Prize.

Chapter Eight

WANGARI MAATHAI AND THE GREEN BELT MOVEMENT

"We should understand nature's laws if we expect her to shower us with earthly blessings. We must stop the over-exploitation and the plundering. We must begin to care."

—*Wangari Maathai*

An African woman trudges up a dusty, yellow hillside. The hot morning sun beats down upon her. On her back, she carries a small bundle of sticks she has gathered. She remembers how, as a child, she used to play here. It was different then. The hill was green with trees and plants. They held the soil together when it rained. Women from her village came here to gather leaves to feed livestock and wood for fires to cook food. Now, there is no greenery left. All is barren. There are only a few short stumps where the last trees once stood. The young woman has come here to try to dig them out of the dusty ground. She needs the wood. Without it, she cannot make a fire for cooking.

The young woman removes the bundle from her back and lays it on the ground. She takes out a large knife. The tip has broken off. It is no good as a knife, but it works fairly well for digging the dusty earth out from around the small stumps. The woman works patiently for more than an hour. She releases first one, then the other stump from the ground. Pleased, she ties the two stumps to her bundle, loads it onto her back and starts off down the hill. As she walks home, she realizes it is not the hot sun that bothers her. It is not the hard work of digging. What bothers her is—what will she do for firewood tomorrow?

Wangari Maathai is working hard to better the lives of African women. She knows that their traditional lifestyle depends upon the land. And, the land is in trouble. This is why she started the Green Belt Movement.

Wangari was born in 1940 in Kenya near the town of Nyeri. Nyeri is near the Great Rift Valley—the place where the first true humans walked upright. Nearby lies the great snow-capped Mount Kenya—the country's highest mountain.

Wangari was born into a rural African village. All of the people in the village were known to her. There were no strangers. She ate traditional foods like maize (a kind of corn), beans, squash and yams. She watched her mother and the women of the village work hard to grow, harvest and prepare the foods that she and the other children ate. There were no computers, no television sets, no microwave ovens. But there was something better. There was a kind of magic in the land.

As a child, Wangari was fond of a huge wild fig tree that grew in the village. Her mother was very protective of that tree. She would not allow anyone to cut it. She would not even allow Wangari to collect the dead twigs from it. The wild fig tree was special. Why? Wangari never knew exactly. Perhaps the tree was special because of all that it had to give—fruit, shade, leaves, wood. But her mother treated the tree as if it were more than just a tree. She treated it as if it were an honored friend. Wangari learned to respect her mother's reverence for the wild fig tree.

The lesson of respect for nature would play an important part in her own life one day.

Wangari enjoyed observing nature. Each day, she drew water from a spring near the fig tree. She was "fascinated by the way the clean, cool water pushed its way through the soft, red clay, so gently that even the individual grains of the soil were left undisturbed."[1] In Wangari's village, people led simple lives. But the water was clean, the children were healthy, and no one went hungry.

Kenya had been under British rule since 1895. In 1960, the United States offered to help prepare Kenya for its coming independence. Scholarships to U.S. colleges were made available to several hundred Kenyan students. Wangari was one of them. She attended Mount St. Scholastica College in Atchison, Kansas. Life in the United States was a big change from what she was used to. For one thing, at home, women were not encouraged to pursue an education. In the United States it was different. Even so, Wangari did not want to remain in the United States. She wanted to return to her

home and share what she had learned. She majored in biology and earned a bachelor of science degree.

In 1965, Wangari received a master of science degree from the University of Pittsburgh. She returned home and became the first woman to receive a doctorate from the University of Nairobi. She also became the University's first woman professor and department chairperson. She was head of the anatomy department.

Wangari married a member of the Kenyan Parliament. They had three children—two boys and a girl. Her husband's district was one of the poorest in Nairobi. Wangari worked to improve conditions for the people there. She tried to create jobs for people so that they could support themselves. The jobs included cleaning up the neighborhood, planting trees and cleaning the homes of wealthy people. There was not always money available to pay the workers. As a result, the project failed. But Wangari knew that the idea of getting people involved to solve their own problems was a good one.

Women's rights was an important issue for Wangari. Wangari's tribal background was Kikuyu. Kikuyu women were permitted to express their opinions and play an important role in society. Not all Kenyans, however, agreed with these values. Something about Wangari bothered her husband, for one. Why was he uneasy about her? Was it because she had a more advanced degree than he did? Was it that she was an outspoken woman? Was it that she was a woman succeeding in a man's academic world? Whatever it was, the couple grew apart and

eventually divorced. "Perhaps I grew up and started getting into the limelight at a time when academic success for a woman was not common," Wangari says. "This put a lot of pressure on a man who was influenced by other men against a successful woman .... But that was in the 1970s—about twenty years ago. I don't think that would have happened now."[2]

After this, Wangari decided to run for Parliament herself. To do this, she resigned from her job at the university. In time, she was told that she would not be permitted to run for parliamentary office. The university refused to take her back. It was a big setback. Wangari, however, turned her disadvantage into an advantage. She focused her attention on planting trees. People said that she was wasting her time and her education. But Wangari did not agree. She felt that she could make a difference.

On June 5—World Environment Day, 1977—Wangari Maathai, together with friends and colleagues, went to the Kamukunji Grounds, a public park, and planted seven trees. With that, the Green Belt Movement was born.

Why the name of Green Belt Movement? Because, says Wangari, people needed to understand how important it was to bring green back to the land. "We wanted to emphasize that by cutting trees, removing vegetation, having this soil erosion, we were literally stripping the Earth of its color," she explains.[3] Why emphasize trees? Because in Kenya, there are few trees left. Less than three percent of Kenya's forests remain.

Loss of trees is a problem because people depend on trees for many things. Trees offer more than shade and beauty. They help to keep the air clean by removing tons of poisonous gases. One of these gases is carbon dioxide. It is produced when people drive cars and trucks that burn gasoline. Trees actually take in carbon dioxide, making the air safer to breathe.

Different trees also give us food in the form of fruit and nuts. They provide habitat for all kinds of animals from insects to birds and small mammals. Trees also reduce soil erosion. (Soil erosion is when the top layer of soil is carried away by wind or other forces. When soil is lost more quickly than new soil can form, it can be a problem. Then the soil that is left is often too poor to grow crops well. Trees can reduce this problem by holding the soil in place with their roots.) Soil erosion is a problem in places like Kenya that have lost many trees.

In Kenya, where many women still cook over an open flame, trees also provide much-needed firewood. Their leaves often provide food for the cows and goats of small farmers. As Wangari Maathai says, "Trees are miracles. They are the best ambassadors for themselves."[4]

Wangari first became aware of the problems caused by loss of trees when she returned from the United States where she had gone to attend college. "When I would visit the village where I was born, I saw whole forests had been cleared for cultivation and timber. People were moving onto hilly slopes and riverbeds ... that were only brush when I was a child. Springs were drying up."[5]

There was also the problem of desertification—the making of desert areas. Desertification happens in places where there is less than average rainfall and where people are forced to use poor soil over and over for planting. Overgrazing of livestock also causes desertification. So does cutting down trees. The soil becomes dry and dusty. Soil erosion becomes a problem too. The wind carries the top layer of soil away. Soil dust in the air makes it harder for air to rise. When the air cannot rise, rain clouds do not form—and there is even less rain.

What is more, changes in the environment had changed how people lived. The people of Wangari's village were not living as well as in the past. For one thing, Wangari noticed that the women were cooking different foods. They were no longer cooking healthy traditional foods like beans and maize. They said that these foods took too long to cook. Cooking them used up too much firewood—which was scarce. Instead the women were buying and cooking refined foods that took less time to cook and used up less wood. But these foods were not healthy. It was bad—especially for children. The children were undernourished, which could lead to sickness. Wangari saw that something needed to be done.

If there were more trees, Wangari knew, firewood would not be a problem. Cooking the healthier, traditional foods would be easy. Trees could help with some of the other problems as well. Springs would be less likely to dry up where there were trees for shade. The process of desertification could be slowed or perhaps even stopped. Wangari saw that trees were the answer to both an environmental problem and a health problem.

Wangari began with the women. In Kenya, as in much of Africa, 80 percent of the farmers are women. Women also keep animals and gather firewood. They are the ones who deal on a daily basis with lack of firewood, poor crops and undernourished children.

She began by bringing in foresters to teach women outside Nairobi how to plant trees. Before long, the women had learned how to gather their own seeds and start seedlings. The seedlings were distributed to women farmers and to schoolchildren. The Green Belt Movement showed the women that if they planted their own trees, they would not have to hunt for firewood. They learned that trees helped hold the soil together, ensuring better crops. In some areas, high winds had swept the roofs off schoolhouses, harming children. So children were brought into the Green Belt Movement as well. They were taught to plant trees around their schools to act as a windbreak.

Thanks to Wangari Maathai, women are learning to plant and care for trees in Kenya and other African nations. In the group's first fifteen years, more than ten million trees have been planted. More than 50,000 women have been involved. One of the secrets of the Green Belt Movement is that it waits to be invited to an area. The people in an area must want it in order for it to work.

Once invited, the group helps women in the area begin their own nursery. It provides hoes and water tanks. It trains and pays a nursery attendant who is chosen by the women. The women are taught to gather seeds from local woodlands and to care for the seedlings in the nursery. When the young trees are big enough, they are given out.

The group pays Green Belt "rangers"— usually elderly or handicapped people—to make sure the seedlings are being cared for. Because of the follow-up, many trees survive. For each tree that lives past a few months, a woman receives one-half a Kenyan shilling. While it is a small amount of money, it makes a difference. The program does more than plant trees. It also gives women a chance to do something important on their own. Receiving even a small amount of money makes the women feel that their work is valued. Improving the land and helping women is what the Green Belt Movement is all about.

Over the years, Wangari Maathai has received many honors for her work with the Green Belt Movement including the Right Livelihood Award (or "alternative Nobel"), the United Nations Environmental Programme Global 500 Award, a "Woman of the World" citation from the Princess of Wales, an honorary degree from Williams College in Massachusetts and the Goldman Environmental Prize.

Eco-Women

In recent years, however, Wangari's work has made her controversial in her home in Kenya. When the Kenyan president wanted to build a 60-story office tower and statue of himself in a Nairobi park, she spoke out against it. She convinced foreign investors that the project was not environmentally friendly. As a result, funding dried up and the project was abandoned. Since then, however, she has been a target of the ruling party. The Green Belt Movement was thrown out of its government offices in downtown Nairobi. And, in 1992, Wangari was clubbed unconscious by police during a protest march. In spite of it all, Wangari continues to work for change and to hope for the future.

"We must never lose hope," says Wangari. "When any of us feels she has an idea or an opportunity, she should go ahead and do it. I never knew when I was working in my backyard that what I was playing around with would one day become a whole movement. One person can make the difference," she says.[6]

Wangari Maathai is the recipient of many honors including the Right Livelihood Award (or "alternative Nobel") and the Goldman Environmental Prize. Copyright © Goldman Environmental Prize.

What You Can Do

1. Write for a free 84-page tree identification pocket guide. You will be sent a guide for trees in your region of the United States. Send your request for "What Tree Is That?" plus your name and address to the National Arbor Day Foundation, Arbor Lodge 100, Nebraska City, NE 68410.

2. Celebrate National Arbor Day in April by planting a tree.

3. Learn more about trees, how they live, and why they are so important. One good resource is *Tree: An Eyewitness Book* by David Burnie (New York: Alfred A. Knopf, 1988).

4. Support the work of the Green Belt Movement, P.O. Box 67545, Nairobi, Kenya. Donations may be made in care of Resource Renewal Institute, Building A, Fort Mason Center, San Francisco, CA 94123. (Checks should be made out to Green Belt International.)

5. See additional suggestions for "What You Can Do" in the chapter on the Chipko Movement of India.

India is a country of colorful marketplaces, crowded city streets and ancient carved stone temples. Copyright © Air-India Slide Library.

Chapter Nine

THE CHIPKO MOVEMENT: EMBRACING TREES

"What do the forests bear?
Soil, water, and pure air."
—*Chipko saying*

The moon rises over a tiny village in the north of India. Terraced gardens slope down to a cluster of small wood houses. Moonlight shines in the window of one house to find a restless little girl. It is past her bedtime, but she is not sleepy. She begs her mother to tell her a story. "Very well," answers her mother. And this is the story that she tells.

"Hundreds of years ago," begins the mother, "our land was ruled by a maharajah. He lived in a white marble palace and was rich and very powerful. Not far from the maharajah's palace, there was a small village. It was the home of Amrita Devi. Near the village there was a beautiful forest. Amrita often visited there. She loved to sit beneath the trees and listen to the song of the wind in their branches.

"One day, Amrita Devi saw a group of men with axes. She followed them to the forest. There, the leader told the others to cut down every last tree. 'It is the maharajah's orders!' he cried. 'These trees will be used to build the new palace.'

"Amrita Devi ran back to her village. When the villagers learned what was happening, they raced to the forest. They begged the axemen not to harm the trees. The trees, said the villagers, gave them the things they needed to live—fuel, food and shelter. But the axemen would not listen. They had their orders.

"Suddenly, Amrita Devi had an idea. She ran to the largest tree and put her arms around it, hugging it. 'Do not cut down our trees,' she cried. 'Without

73

them, we cannot live.' When they saw what she was doing, the other villagers did the same. The axemen could not cut the trees without harming the villagers.

"Do you know what?" the mother asks her daughter. "Today, hundreds of years later, people are still hugging trees to save them from being cut down." But the little girl does not hear her mother. She has fallen asleep and dreams that she is the brave Amrita Devi leading her people to save the trees.

The legendary Amrita Devi was one of the earliest known eco-women. In India today, women are still embracing the trees in order to protect them. These women call themselves the Chipko Movement. Their name, *chipko*, means "to hug."

India is a country of rich and varied extremes—a land of noisy, crowded marketplaces; silent temples carved in stone; women in graceful, flowing saris; and city streets packed with cars, bicycles, ox-carts, cows and rickshaws. It is the Taj Mahal, the ancient Elephant Caves and the grimy slums of Calcutta. It is wealth, opulence and beauty side by side with grim poverty.

India is a land of contrasts in its climate and geography too. The south is hot, yet the north is temperate—with warm days and cool nights. Much of India is flat plains, but not in the north where the Himalayan Mountains run in a vast, majestic line. At one time, the land of the Himalaya was dense with trees. A western explorer described it as "an enchanted garden" rich with fruit trees, shrubs and flowers.[1] Since that time, many trees have been cut down.

India is a large, diverse country. It is about one-third the size of the United States with about three and one-half times as many people. Overpopulation is one of India's many challenges. Although the official language is Hindi, sixteen languages are spoken including English. About 80 percent of the people are Hindus. There are also Moslems, Christians, Sikhs and Buddhists.

In the early 1600s, the British East India Company gained a foothold in India when it set up trading stations there. The British were eager for spices that came to India by trade routes from the east. Over the next two centuries, the British East India Company gained control of most of the country.

During the 1800s, European nations claimed many developing nations for themselves. It was the age of colonialism. The Europeans made "colonies" of other lands such as India and Africa. Great Britain officially took over governing India in 1858. For decades, educated Indians called for self-rule. But there was little change.

In the 1920s and 1930s, political activists such as Mahatma Gandhi and Jawaharlal Nehru became popular. They worked hard for Indian independence. Gandhi, in particular, encouraged people to resist British rule peacefully. He did not ask that Indians fight the British—simply that they not cooperate. He helped people organize. He called for workers to stop working all at the same time—for a day or more. This made it difficult for the government to get anything done. Gandhi called what he was doing *nonviolent resistance.* It got him into a lot of trouble with British authorities and he was jailed many times.

Great Britain finally granted independence to India in 1947. Independence, however, came at a price. Many people lost their lives in riots and fighting. Gandhi himself, a man who had worked for peace all his life, was shot and killed by an extremist. His principles of nonviolent resistance, however, were carried on by his followers. In time, these followers, many of them women, influenced others who became the Chipko Movement.

One of Gandhi's followers, Mira Behn, lived in a village in the north of India. Here, the Ganga River flows out from the foot of the Himalayan Mountains. This river is sacred to many Hindus. One year, Mira Behn witnessed a terrible flood.

> … as the swirling waters increased, [there] came first bushes and boughs and great logs of wood, then in the turmoil of more and more water came whole trees, cattle of all sizes and from time to time a human being clinging to the remnants of his hut. Nothing could be done to save man or beast from this turmoil; the only hope was for them to get caught up somewhere on the edge of an island or riverbank.[2]

Mira Behn wondered what had caused such a dangerous flood. She explored the area north of her village. She discovered that thousands of trees had been cut down. In some places, the forest was bare. In others,

The Ganga, a major river in India, begins its journey at the foot of the Himalayan Mountains. The river is sacred to Hindus, many of whom travel here to the crowded city of Banaras to worship at least once in their lives. Copyright © Air-India Library.

the land had been replanted with pine trees. Quick-growing pine trees could be cut and sold. They made fine sporting goods equipment for people in other countries like the United States. But they did not protect the land the way the trees that had once grown here had done. They were of no use to the mountain people who lived here.

Old oak trees had once held this soil together. Now that they were gone, the soil broke apart and washed away easily. There were landslides. With nothing to hold the water back, heavy rains brought terrible flooding. Many people and animals lost their lives. One such terrible flood took place in 1970. Commercial logging was the cause. After that, people in the mountain villages began to organize.

The Chipko Movement came to life one morning in March 1973 in the village of Mandal. Earlier, the government had granted a factory owner the right to cut ash trees in the forest of Mandal. The villagers were against cutting the trees. They said they would not allow the trees to be cut down. In the end, the factory owner gave up on the ash trees. Not a single tree was cut.

The encounter was the first of its kind. Until then, the government had pretty much done what it wanted with the forests. This was the first time that poor villagers had stood up and said "no!" The encounter was unusual for another reason. Many of the villagers who protested cutting the trees were women. In traditional Indian society, poor women have little say in how things are done. By joining together, however, the women had made a difference.

Before long, though, the factory owner got permission to cut trees elsewhere—in a place called Kedar Ghati. Women from nearby villages began walking to this forest. As they walked, more women from other villages joined them. The villagers camped out in the forest. They sang songs and chanted Chipko slogans. The loggers could not get anywhere. Finally, they gave up and went home.

The following year, the government auctioned off trees in a place called Reni. The government arranged for the men of Reni village to be away on the day the loggers were to arrive. The men were told to go to another town to receive money that was due them. With the men out of the way, the loggers proceeded to the forest.

A little girl was tending the village cattle. Suddenly, she saw the loggers' bus on its way to the forest. She rushed to a woman named Gaura Devi. Gaura Devi was a widow in her 50s and a respected leader in the village. She called the women of the village together. A group of them headed for the forest.

When they arrived there, they found that some of the loggers had been drinking alcohol. One of them pointed a gun at Gaura Devi. "Shoot us," she is reported as saying in a calm, steady voice. "Only then will you be able to cut down this forest."[3] The loggers felt ashamed. They left the forest without cutting a single tree.

The Chipko Movement began to gather strength. People traveled from one hill town to the next. They spoke to the villagers about protecting their forests. They told of how others had come up against loggers and wealthy contractors—and won. The villagers saw that by joining together, they could protect their trees.

Many women became part of the Chipko Movement. Why? Perhaps because trees were important to them. In the hill towns of India, the lifestyle is very traditional. Many people live as their ancestors did long ago. For generations, women here have been responsible for growing crops. Leaves from trees are used as fertilizer for planting. It is women who have the job of cooking food and of gathering firewood to cook it over open fires. In times when food is scarce, the forest also yields mushrooms and other good things to eat. Women also tend livestock—and certain leaves are used to feed cows. Without the trees, these women knew their work would be harder. They and their families would suffer. The Chipko Movement gave women a way to protect not only the trees, but their way of life.

Some men also became involved with the Chipko Movement. The person who first came up with the idea of hugging trees was a man named Chandi Prasad Bhatt. He grew up in a small village in the mountains. He understood the link between logging and floods. He was also a believer in the nonviolent philosophy of Mahatma Gandhi. He has been part of the Chipko Movement for a long time, as has Sunderlal Bahuguna. For years, Bahuguna has traveled from village to village, encouraging people to take control of and protect their forests. The villagers appreciate that he lives like they do, has little money and is motivated by concern for people and the land—not profit. When Bahuguna talks about protecting the forests, the villagers listen.

The Chipko Movement continued to grow. Marches were organized. One march lasted for 75 days. The marches drew attention to the problems caused by cutting too many trees.

In 1977, trees in the forest of Adwani were marked for cutting. Women from fifteen villages gathered together. They promised to protect the forest. For days, they walked among the trees, tying sacred threads to the branches in honor of that promise. They had argued with the forestry officer who had visited their village. He had said the trees would provide timber and bring money into the Indian economy. They answered that the forest yields soil, water and pure air—the basis of life itself. Upon seeing the large number of protesters, the loggers departed.

The loggers, however, were not gone for good. They returned several months later, arriving in trucks and accompanied by the police. They were met by 500 villagers, many of them women. A number of women had children with them. Men armed with rifles walked up and down in an effort to scare the villagers away. The women were tense. Their children watched with wide, frightened eyes. No one moved.

The loggers piled out of the trucks. They were told to get to work and ignore the crowd. But when they entered the forest, the women and children did too. As each logger went up to a tree, three or four women encircled it. They explained that they needed the trees in order to live. The loggers could do nothing.

The police were puzzled. Why weren't the women afraid of the guns? Why didn't they run away? The police could have arrested the women, but there was no jail big enough to hold so many. After some time, the frustrated contractor called off the effort. The loggers and the police went home. The villagers had won.

This same scene was played out in many more villages and many more forests. In time, government officials came to see the Chipko Movement as a force to be reckoned with.

The question is the same everywhere. Should people sell their natural resources to bring money into their economy? Or, should the resources be left for people to use? The women of the Chipko Movement say that such a choice is no choice at all. Without trees, they will have no firewood for their cooking, no fodder for their livestock, no fertilizer for their crops and less food for their children. The gifts of the forest, they say, should be enjoyed by all.

In 1987, the Chipko Movement received the Right Livelihood Award. Often called the "alternative Nobel," this award is presented

Sunderlal Bahuguna and Indu Tikekar receive the Right Livelihood Award. Copyright © Per Frisk, courtesy Right Livelihood Awards.

each year in Stockholm on the day before the Nobel Prize is given. It draws worldwide attention to those whose work is helping to heal our planet and uplift humanity. The Right Livelihood Award was given to the Chipko Movement "for showing how the forests of Himalaya and the world can be saved."[4]

WHAT YOU CAN DO

1. Share the legend of Amrita Devi. Read aloud with younger students the picturebook *The People Who Hugged the Trees* by Deborah Lee Rose (Roberts Rinehart Publishers, Box 666, Niwot, CO 80544).

2. Plant a tree. Write for your own student tree-planting kit from Trees for Life, 1103 Jefferson, Wichita, KS 67203-3599. A classroom kit is also available. Ask them about their campaign to plant trees in India.

3. Ask your family to get involved in tree planting in your community. One resource is the book *Growing Greener Cities* available for $10.95 postpaid from American Forests, 1516 P Street NW, Washington, D.C. 20005.

4. If your family celebrates Christmas, use a live tree instead of one that is cut. For ideas on how to do this (and other great ways to help the environment) see *50 Simple Things Kids Can Do to Save the Earth* by the EarthWorks Group, 1400 Shattuck #25, Berkeley, CA 94709.

5. See additional suggestions for "What You Can Do" in the chapter on Wangari Maathai and the Green Belt Movement.

AFTERWORD

What do the women in this book have in common? A dream for a better world, a willingness to work hard, a desire to make a difference for our planet and its people and animals. The experiences of these women are important if only because they remind us that we are not alone, that others have gone before us. These are extraordinary individuals. And yet their example bears witness that everyone can follow a dream, work hard and influence our world for the better.

Suggestions are offered at the end of each chapter of this volume for simple actions anyone can take to learn more and help the Earth. Don't stop there. Let your imagination guide you as you seek new ways to help protect our environment. From the Children's Earth Summit to the Tree Musketeers of El Segundo, California, young people from one end of our nation to the other are joining together to help heal the planet. Get involved. Find out what you can do.

What of other eco-women whose stories are not told here? What of Helena Norberg-Hodge helping the Ladakh people to improve their environment while maintaining their traditional culture? What of ecologist Christine Jean, known as "Madame Loire," working to save France's longest river? What of ethologists Biruté Galdikas and Dian Fossey, or Margaret Morse Nice who was described by her biographer as the founder of ethology?

The more we listen and learn, the more questions we uncover that beg to be answered. There are more eco-women with stories worth telling than can possibly find their way into a single volume. As you encounter them in your reading and studies, be open to their stories, their challenges, their courage. May their example inspire us all to listen more closely, work more patiently and share the Earth more fully.

NOTES

CHAPTER 1

1. *Rachel Carson* by Marty Jezer. New York: Chelsea House Publishers, 1988, page 26.
2. Letter from Rachel Carson to the Cat Welfare Association, quoted in *The House of Life: Rachel Carson at Work* by Paul Brooks. Boston: Houghton Mifflin, 1972, page 33.
3. Jezer, page 29.
4. Brooks, page 1.
5. *Sea and Earth: The Life of Rachel Carson* by Philip Sterling. New York: Thomas Y. Crowell, 1970, page 135.
6. *Rachel Carson: The Wonder of Nature* by Catherine Reef, illustrated by Larry Raymond. New York: Twenty-First Century Books, 1991, page 53.
7. Ibid., page 65.

CHAPTER 2

1. *Florida: The Long Frontier* by Marjory Stoneman Douglas. New York: Harper & Row, 1967, page 3.
2. *The Everglades: River of Grass* by Marjory Stoneman Douglas. New York: Rinehart, 1947, page 1.
3. *Marjory Stoneman Douglas: Voice of the River* by Marjory Stoneman Douglas. Sarasota, FL: Pineapple Press, 1987, page 190.
4. Ibid., page 227.
5. Author's taped interview, March 1991.
6. Author's taped interview, December 1993.
7. Author's taped interview, March 1991.

CHAPTER 3

1. *Bearing Witness* by Gertrude Blom. Chapel Hill: University of North Carolina Press, 1984, page 8.
2. Ibid., page 145.
3. Ibid., page 11.
4. Gertrude Blom quoted in documentary *Gertrude Blom: Guardian of the Rain Forest,* produced and directed by Robert S. Cozens, distributed by Filmmakers Library, New York, NY.
5. Blom, quoted in documentary above.

Chapter 4

1. *In the Shadow of Man* by Jane Van Lawick-Goodall. Boston: Houghton Mifflin, 1971, page 268.
2. Jane Goodall, *Through a Window*. Boston: Houghton Mifflin, 1990, page 14.

Chapter 5

1. Letter from Barbara Prosser Kerr to the author dated November 11, 1994.
2. Ibid.
3. Ibid.
4. Letter from Barbara Prosser Kerr to the author dated May 26, 1994.
5. Letter, dated November 11, 1994.
6. Ibid.
7. *Changing Lives with the Sun,* video produced by Barbara Kerr and Sherry Cole, 1988.
8. *The Expanding World of Solar Box Cookers* by Barbara Prosser Kerr. Taylor, AZ: self-published, 1991, page 2.
9. Ibid., page 39.
10. Letter, dated November 11, 1994.
11. Letter, dated May 26, 1994.

Chapter 6

1. "Picking Up Mammals' Deep Notes" by Jane Brody. *The New York Times*, November 9, 1993, pages C1 and C15.
2. *Elephants Calling* by Katharine Payne. New York: Crown, 1992, page 11.
3. Ibid., page 12.
4. Ibid., page 20.
5. Ibid., page 36.

Chapter 7

1. *Two in the Far North* by Margaret Murie. New York: Alfred A. Knopf, 1962, page 97.
2. Ibid., page 95.
3. Ibid., page 143.
4. Quote from Margaret Murie, courtesy of Bonnie Kreps.

Chapter 8

1. *Eco-Heroes: Twelve Tales of Environmental Victory* by Aubrey Wallace. San Francisco: Mercury House, 1993, page 10.
2. "Empowering the Voiceless" from *West Africa Magazine*, September 30–October 6, 1991.
3. "The Greening of Kenya" by Louise Sweeney. *Christian Science Monitor*, October 7, 1986
4. "Healing the Ravaged Land" by Maryanne Vollers. *International Wildlife*, 1988, page 17.
5. Ibid., page 17.
6. "Foresters without Diplomas" by Wangari Maathai. *Ms.* magazine, March/April 1991, page 75.

Chapter 9

1. *Excursions in India* by Thomas Skinner published in 1832, quoted in *The Unquiet Woods: Ecological Change and Peasant Resistance in the Himalaya* by Ramachandra Guha. Berkeley: University of California Press, 1990, page 9.
2. *Staying Alive* by Vandana Shiva. Atlantic Highlands, NJ: Zed Books Ltd., 1989, page 69.
3. *This River of Courage* by Pam McAllister. Philadelphia: New Society Publishers, 1991, page 49.
4. "The Right Livelihood Award," brochure, 1994, courtesy of the Right Livelihood Awards Administrative Office, P.O. Box 15072, S-10465 Stockholm, Sweden.

INDEX